The Bandit Kings of the Cookson Hills

By R.D. Morgan

NEW FORUMS PRESS INC.

Stillwater, Okla., U.S.A.

NEW FORUMS PRESS INC.

Published in the United States of America
by New Forums Press, Inc.
1018 S. Lewis St.
Stillwater, OK 74074
www.newforums.com

Library of Congress Cataloging-in-Publication Data Pending

This book may be ordered in bulk quantities at discount from New
Forums Press, Inc., P.O. Box 876, Stillwater, OK 74076 [Federal
I.D. No. 73 1123239]. Printed in the United States of America.

ISBN 10: 1581070829; ISBN 13: 978-1581070828

Cover Photos
Top: Bush Wood, courtesy Dian Schwanz.
Bottom, left to right: Cowboys of the Cookson Hills; Henry Starr
after being wounded in Stroud shootout, courtesy *Stroud Messenger*; Cherokee Bill, courtesy Ft. Smith Historic Site.

Foreword

Many volumes have been written about America's outlaw past, but rarely from the proper perspective. Few writers have grasped the very real connection between the desperadoes of the "Old West" and bank robbing Midwest gangsters of the 1930s. The connection is real, a direct line of criminal descent can be traced from Quantrell and the James boys in the 1860s down to John Dillinger, and "Pretty Boy" Floyd in the 1930s, as men drifted from one gang to another over the seventy-year period. Yet most outlaw and lawmen researchers focus on one extreme end of the period or the other, either the horseback bandits or the tommy-gunning bank marauders of the Depression era. Frontier outlaw buffs tend to close their narratives with the Daltons' disastrous 1892 raid on Coffeyville, Kansas or with the celebrated exploits of Butch Cassidy and his "Wild Bunch." Writers on the "Dillinger days" often see the 1930s crime wave as a modern phenomenon resulting from the Prohibition and the Depression. A serious gap in American criminal history has prevailed until now, for in between were those transitionary figures, largely ignored in the great mass of crime literature, who spanned both periods, as the age of the horse and six-shooter gave way to that of the automobile and the automatic pistol.

Oklahoma writer R. D. Morgan has effectively bridged this gap with his books. It's fertile territory for research, as no other state in the union has a richer and bloodier outlaw history. In *Armed and Dangerous*, Morgan presented a miscellany of Oklahoma crime stories from the '20s and '30s covering the exploits of noted outlaws and lawmen alike. With *The Bad Boys of the Cookson Hills*, he told the full story of a murderous band of Depression bank robbers. He went back to the World War I period in *Desperadoes*, with the history of the Poe-Hart gang, a short-lived, but deadly combination of horse thieves-turned-automotive-bandits. He brings it full circle now with this "prequel," bridging the "Wild West" with 20th Century crime.

Henry Starr, a product of one of the Southwest's most infamous outlaw families, began his career of crime in the 1890s, a contemporary of the Daltons, Bill Doolin, Cherokee Bill and Al Jennings. Between several prison terms and a few half-hearted attempts at rehabilitation (including a brief and unprofitable stint playing himself in silent Westerns), Starr by his own declaration "robbed more banks than any man in America" before going down ingloriously in a 1921 bank robbery in Harrison, Arkansas. He turned "snitch" on his deathbed, naming his confederates. The remnants of Starr's gang aligned with other criminals in Eastern Oklahoma in the early 1920s and succeeded Henry and his predecessors as the new "Bandit Kings of the Cookson Hills." Among them was a mysterious "Fagin" in his seventies or thereabouts known as John "Kaiser Bill" Goodman, probably not his real name, who had a string of prison terms under various aliases dating back years and boasted of having once ridden with the Dalton Gang.

A wild and heavily timbered region—the Oklahoma side of the Ozarks—the Cooksons had long served as a base of banditry. Populated largely by impoverished Indians and clannish hill families with little use for banks and railroads and little respect for law and order from the outside world, it was a haven for those on the run, a sanctuary for moonshiners and robbers and a hostile otherworld for those who wore a tin star. Men like Ed Lockhart, Mount Cookson (a descendent of one of the regions pioneers), Bush Wood, the Price brothers and their associates, along with the younger upstarts like the Kimes brothers and Charles "Pretty Boy" Floyd, grew up in an outlaw tradition, hearing about the Daltons, Bill Doolin and the "Verdigris Kid" from old-timers who remembered them. Lockhart's band was the original Cookson Hills Gang of the 1920s, the forerunner of the Carlile-Bradshaw-Underhill gang of the depression era and included some of the same members such as "Kie" Carlile, Mount Cookson, Charlie Cotner, and even old "Kaiser Bill." They may be largely forgotten elsewhere but in the Hills of Eastern Oklahoma and Western Arkansas, their names and exploits are still legendary.

R. D. Morgan is well qualified to tell the story. A transplanted Iowa farm boy who grew up in that not too distant time some of us still recall when well-water, clotheslines, coal bins, and outhouses were still fairly common and microwave ovens, cable T.V., credit cards, home computers, and cell phones were undreamed of, he has a county boys instincts and a passion for the simpler times of our rural past. Combine this with an objective journalistic bent, a nice feel for the literary style of ancient detective magazines, a researchers dedication to getting the facts straight, and some law enforcement experience, and it's an unbeatable combination. As in his previous books, Morgan praises the efforts of the brave lawmen that tracked the outlaws against formidable odds over hostile terrain and the equally brave efforts of citizen vigilantes but does not hesitate to relate episodes unflattering to the protagonists on either side of the law. This is a guy who just wants to set the record straight. And this is one helluva book and an important contribution to lawmen and outlaw history.

Rick Mattix
Author of *Public Enemies:*
America's Criminal Past, 1919-1940

Table of Contents

To Naomi

... my loving companion and tireless supporter, my Mother, who first opened my eyes to the magical world of books, and Uncle Lyle, may we meet again in the Powder River Country.

Acknowledgements

I wish to express my gratitude to my wife Naomi, my publisher, Doug Dollar, Dian Schwanz and members of the Wood, Lockhart, Kimes, and Dotson families, along with Rick Mattix, Kenneth Butler, Henry Jolliff, Janet Baker, Julie Arrowood, Arthur Thompson, June Westphal, Fred Gossett, Bruce Williams, Greta Stephenson, Rose Nicholson, Luther Gregory Junior, Mary Bowser, Jim Reiff, Joe Tucker, Pamela Crutchfield, Ida Works, Joe Kelley, Tom Ballenger, and finally, the many residents of Oklahoma's Cookson Hills who tolerated my constant badgering for the past three years. Without them all, this book could not of been written.

About the Author

R. D. Morgan is the author of four nonfiction books dealing with early day Oklahoma lawmen and outlaws. He has also written numerous articles for Oklahoma newspapers and historical magazines on the subject.

Morgan spent his childhood in the East Texas oil patch country and his teen years living in a small Iowa farming community. Upon graduation from high school, he knocked around a year or so working construction before entering the U.S. Army where he served as a law enforcement officer. After his military career, he attended the College of the Ozarks before being employed as an electrician and maintenance supervisor for many years in Missouri and Arkansas. On retirement, he moved to Oklahoma to fulfill his lifelong desire to commit his energies full-time into writing and researching depression era American history. Morgan developed a passion for the subject as a teenager listening to his Grandfather's tales of life and culture in Middle America during the 1920-30s. Morgan and his wife Naomi presently reside in Eastern Oklahoma. He is currently working on several projects with author, researcher Rick "Maddog" Mattix, including the story of the infamous "Ma" Barker Gang, as well as the saga of the notorious Wilber Underhill.

Preface

This book chronicles the true adventures of a loose-knit confederation of daring bank bandits originating from the infamous Cookson Hills of Eastern Oklahoma who terrorized the Arkansas-Oklahoma borderlands for more than a half decade following the close of the First World War.

The original leader of the group was Henry Starr, the Cherokee bandit, who claimed to have robbed more banks than any man. Upon his death, a middle-age store-keeper along with an audacious young war hero named Ed Lockhart took over the helm.

In a time when most Americans were captivated by the "Teapot Dome" scandal, the death of President Harding, and the gridiron adventures of Notre Dame's "Four Horsemen," as well as Rudolf Valintino's breath-less portrayal as "the Sheik" on the silver screen, folks living in the Ozark Mountains watched with fear and fas-cination as the outlaw band committed their bold depra-vations. Although the gang's take rarely amounted to over $2000, it must be remembered the average yearly income for a family of five in 1922 amounted to $2100. A gallon of gas cost eleven-cents and a loaf of bread fetched only nine pennies. A man could buy a new car for $300, and a decent home for a couple of grand or less.

The outlaw horde eventually met their match when they collided with such notable lawmen as Mont Grady, the Choctaw Indian manhunter with nerves of steel, and Cherokee County Deputies Jay Fellows and Jerry Powell, who rode horseback forty-eight hours in blizzard conditions without the benefit of food or rest in a dogged pursuit of the lawbreakers.

Although members of the bandit gang received a great deal of notoriety from their illicit adventures, it was these officers and the ordinary citizens of towns such as Eureka Springs, Arkansas and Stroud, Oklahoma who took up arms and fought the outlaws to a standstill, who proved to be the real heroes of the story.

This account, which takes place in the "Roaring '20s," is meant to serve as a prelude to my first book, *The Bad Boys of the Cookson Hills*, which chronicled the activities of another band of outlaws who launched a prolific series of attacks on nearly two-dozen banks in Kansas, Oklahoma, Nebraska, and Arkansas during the 1930s depression era. This second "Cookson Hills" Gang was headquartered in the same geographic area as the earlier version noted in this narrative and some of the characters involved with the original outfit were active members of the latter group.

"I never intended to be taken alive."
Ed Lockhart to Sheriff Ben Smith, Jay, Oklahoma 1923.

"Scouting":
a phrase dating from frontier times, which implies
running from or dodging the law.

"Robbing people with a six-gun,
I fought the law and the law won,
Now I'm breaking rocks in the hot sun."
– Bobby Fuller – Mustang Music - 1965

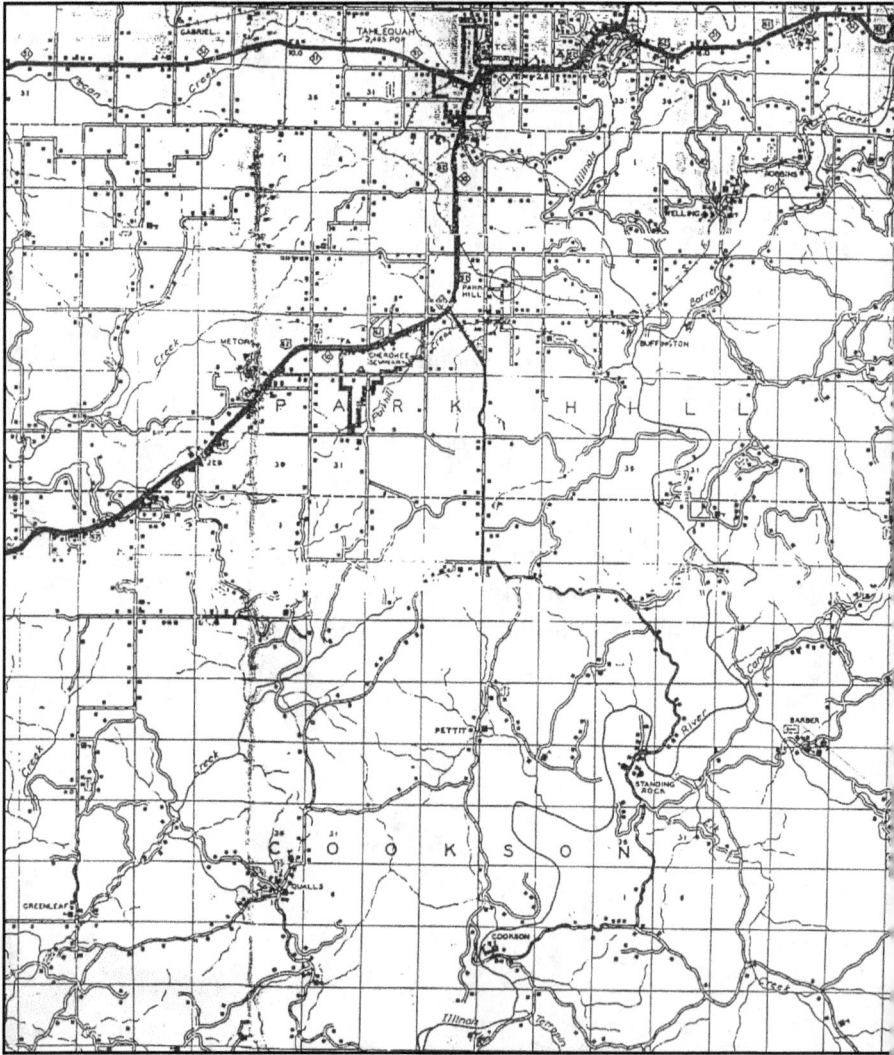

Detailed road map of the Cookson Hills district circa 1925 Map courtesy of Northeastern State University, Tahlequah, Oklahoma.

Chapter 1

Armed Robbery

10:00 am, February 18, 1921:

On a cold, overcast Friday morning, a late model Nash automobile loaded down with four men, parked directly in front of the Peoples National Bank, located on the southwest corner of the courthouse square in the northern Arkansas community of Harrison, Arkansas. Three of the individuals quickly bolted from the rig making a bee-line for the financial institution's front door, while the fourth sat at the wheel with the motor running.

After entering the bank, the unmasked trio, armed with handguns, fanned out. The lead bandit, described as an Indian, approached the cashier, G. C. "Cleve" Coffman, loudly stating, "Stick 'em up, and be damned snappy," adding "You work with me and I'll work with you." All seven witnesses and employees froze with fear, except one. Sixty-nine-year-old William J. Myers, a bank director, slipped unseen into the shadows of a walk-in vault where he located a .38 caliber model '73 Winchester rifle which had long ago been placed there for just this sort of emergency.

After cleaning out the cash drawers to the tune of nearly $3000 in paper money, which he stuffed in a burlap bag, the robber doing the talking ordered the terrified cash-

William J. Myer. Courtesy Daily Oklahoman.

ier to open the safe. As the bandit leaned down to observe the cashier work the safe's spindle a thunderous noise rang out. The Indian, clutching his side, hit the floor where he laid withering in agony as the steel-nerved Myers, intent on finishing the job, chambered another round. As the elderly bank director stepped out of the vault, the gravely wounded outlaw began pleading with him not to "Shoot a man while he's down!"

Observing their wounded comrade slip to the floor, his two companions swiftly backed out the door. One of them seized a witness, Miss Ruth Wilson, using her as a human shield. On reaching the running car, the pair released the woman and jumped into the rig while pleading with the driver to "Move it."

Meanwhile, Myers ran into the street firing a barrage of rounds at the fleeing car, puncturing a tire and shattering the rear window. The bandits returned fire, their rounds all going astray hitting a park bench and roadside curb.

A few miles south of town, the robbers abandoned the Nash setting fire to the car's roof before fleeing on foot into the nearby timber. Several carloads of armed citizens in hot pursuit found the car engulfed in flames in the center of the road near a railway underpass. Although the automobile was discovered without license plates, several witnesses swore they had observed Oklahoma tags on the car while it was parked in front of the bank.

"The Bearcat"
Henry Starr.
Author's private collection.

After dousing the flames, the posse, which had grown considerably in size, began searching the adjacent woods for any sign of the bandits. When darkness set in, the vigilantes gave up the manhunt and drifted back to town.

Town square Harrison, Arkansas at time of the robbery; courthouse left front, arrow pointing to Peoples Bank. Courtesy of the Tulsa Tribune.

Lawmen guessed the fugitives may have arranged for several horses to be tethered in the thick forest enabling them to make their escape. Adding to the confusion was the fact the outlaws had cut the phone lines leading out of town earlier that day.

Back at the bank, several men were recruited to carry the wounded bandit, who had turned a ghostly white and was shrieking in pain, to a cot located in a cell in the nearby Boone County Jail. As of yet, no one could guess the identity of the desperado. A few hours following the robbery, the gravely wounded bandit requested to talk to George Crump, a local man who had once served as a Federal Marshal. He was not available, but his son came by the jail. On glancing at the agonized figure lying on the cot, young Crump immediately recognized the man, saying: "Why that is Henry Starr!"

In the long bloody history of banditry in Oklahoma and the Indian Territory, no man had made his mark more boldly than Henry Starr. The noted highwayman (nicknamed "The Bearcat") once

HENRY STARR SHOT IN RAID AT HARRISON

Notorious Bandit Wounded Attempting to Rob Bank.

BANKER FIRES SHOT

W. J. Myers Outwits Robbers and Saves $30,000 in Deposits.

WOUNDED MAN MAY DIE

Arkansas Gazette
February 19, 1921

News clipping. Courtesy of the Arkansas Gazette.

made the claim he had robbed more banks than any man living or dead. It was not an idle boast. Modern historians estimate the daring outlaw stuck up between ten and twenty financial institutions, four rail depots, and a score of small general stores in his long career.

The picturesque outlaw, who was the nephew of the notorious Belle Starr, was born of Indian parentage near Fort Gibson, Cherokee Nation in 1873. He began his lengthy career in crime in 1891 when he was charged with introducing liquor into the Territory. Ironically, he swore to his dying day he was innocent of that particular crime. Following this incident, he robbed a pair of area stores and a rail depot in Nowata. When a Federal Marshal named Floyd Wilson caught up with the miscreant near Lenapah on December 14, 1892, Starr shot him dead in a short but ferocious gun battle. Legend has it, that at the conclusion of the deadly duel, the nervy outlaw approached the dying Deputy informing him; "You should've left well enough alone and minded your own business." The following year, he and several companions began an extensive crime spree starting with the looting of a trio of rail stations at Pryor Creek, Choteau, and Inola, Indian Territory, before raiding the banks of Caney, Kansas and Bentonville, Arkansas.

On July 3, 1893, the audacious bandit, along with his girlfriend and crime partner "Kid" Wilson, were captured at a swanky cafe in Colorado Springs, Colorado spending their ill-gotten gains on a sumptuous feast of oysters and crawfish. The duo, minus their attractive lady friend, were promptly extradited to the jurisdiction of "Hanging Judge" Isaac Parker in Fort Smith, Arkansas. After a short trial, Parker sentenced Starr to hang from the neck until dead for the murder of Marshal Wilson. A few months after Henry's death sentence was meted out, the US Supreme Court overturned Parker's verdict and granted the young Indian a chance at a new trial.

Around the time Henry's retrial was scheduled to begin, the infamous "Cherokee Bill," who was being housed in a cell near Starr's, went on a shooting rampage with a pistol which had been smuggled into the jail. The convicted murderer kept the entire jailhouse under siege for several hours, eventually killing a guard

Judge Parker. Courtesy Fort Smith Historic Site.

named Larry Keating before Starr, in an act of incredible courage, strolled into Bill's cell and talked the murderous thug into surrendering his weapon. "Bill," who was noted as a pitiless, "cold-blooded son of a bitch" swung from the Fort Smith gallows on the afternoon of March 17, 1896, to no one's regret. Incidentally, when the hangman asked the outlaw if he had any last words, he loudly proclaimed, "I came here to die,

Cherokee Bill. Courtesy Fort Smith Historic Site.

Grave of Cherokee Bill, (Crawford Goldsby) Fort Gibson, Oklahoma. Photo by Naomi Morgan.

not make a speech." The bandit's body was transported by rail back to his hometown of Fort Gibson, Indian Territory a few days after his execution and buried in the public bone yard.

Several months following the botched jailhouse uprising, Starr was retried for the murder of Deputy Wilson and for a second time convicted and sentenced to hang. In early 1897, the US Supreme Court again overturned Parker's (who had since died) death sentence ordering a new trial in Henry's case. On his third retrial, Starr was allowed to plead guilty to manslaughter and robbery. Judge John Rogers sentenced him to fifteen years in the Federal Penitentiary at Columbus, Ohio, as inmate #30246. After serving only four years in the big house, President Theodore Roosevelt, who secretly admired the image of the western bad man of book and lore, foolishly offered the errant outlaw executive clemency. Roosevelt's only stipulation was to demand the bandit give his word of honor that he would sin no more. Starr, who was no more capable of traveling the straight and narrow than a wiggling rattlesnake, readily agreed to the chief executive's overly romanticized terms.

After his release, Henry married and was blessed with a son, who the couple named Theodore Roosevelt Starr in honor of his benefactor. To his credit, Starr, who proclaimed himself "fully reformed," somehow managed to stay out of trouble until 1908 when he teamed back up with his ex-partner, "Kid" Wilson, who had recently been paroled from prison. Within a month's time, the duo robbed both the banks of Tyro, Kansas and Amity, Colorado. In November of the same year, the outlaw was arrested in Arizona and extradited to Colorado where he was convicted of the Amity job. Facing a seven to twenty-five-year sentence, the famed bad man settled down and wrote his autobiography titled "Thrilling Events." After

Modern-day view of old Carney State Bank, Carney, Oklahoma. Photo by Naomi Morgan.

nearly five years of being a model prisoner, Starr was paroled back to society on September 24, 1913. In the interim, his wife, disgusted with Henry's raucous ways, had divorced him and went her own way.

Over the next two years, Starr, returning to his previous life as the self-proclaimed "boldest bandit on the Arkansas River," was suspected of robbing nearly a dozen banks in Oklahoma. One of those holdups took place on December 29, 1914 at the Carney State Bank located in Lincoln County, Oklahoma. Old-timer Harry Dobson, who witnessed the raid standing in a barbershop across the street from the financial institution, described the affair to a reporter from the *Tulsa World* many decades after the event saying, "I can remember it almost like it was yesterday when Henry Starr and Lewis Estes walked up to the bank. Starr entered the bank while Estes covered him outside. Having trouble with a group of elderly freeloaders sitting whittling on a bench located in front of the bank, Estes told the group, 'I'm not fooling around, Ya'll move out of here. Were robbing this place." According to Dobson, the squatters didn't seem very impressed with the gunman till he slammed his hat down and began menacingly waving his Winchester in the air. Dobson stated, "I guess the old-timers figured he might pull the trigger by accident cause they all got up and moved down to the next bench." After looting the business for several hundred dollars, Starr joined his partner in the street pushing a bank clerk and several customers in front of him toward a corral where the bandit's horses were tied. One of the customers was a man named Herman Stump, who Dobson described as, "A 5x5 man, five feet tall and five feet wide and weighing about 300 pounds." Dobson claimed he heard Starr order the hostages to put their hands in their pockets, to which Stump responded he couldn't find his pockets and hadn't been able to in years. Starr chuckled and told the big man to keep moving. According to Dobson, Stump again protested, telling the outlaw "This isn't fair you boys making a man of my girth do all this walking, it's hard on me." Starr just grinned, and taking a bag of silver dollars from his belt flung them to the oversized fellow telling him to "Take this and go back and keep your mouth shut." Upon reaching their horses, the bandits mounted and thanked the citizens for their courtesy before riding off in the sunset. Poor Mr. Stump returned the silver dollars to the bank and reportedly retreated to his residence totally exhausted from his taxing experience.

Three months later, on the morning of March 27, 1915, Starr and seven others journeyed to the small Oklahoma town of Stroud on horseback. On reaching the village's business district, they rode to the community stockyards where the group dismounted and left their horses in the care of Henry's longtime pal, Bud Maxfield. Splitting up into two smaller groups; Starr and two others walked to the nearby Stroud National Bank, while the rest of the party led by Lewis Estes entered the First National, located a block away.

Ironically, on approaching the Stroud National Bank, Henry noticed a large placard hanging in the bank's win-

Site of First National Bank now a tag office. Photo by Naomi Morgan.

dow offering a reward of $1000 (Dead or Alive) for the capture of Henry Starr. After cracking a wide smile, the outlaw and a companion named Charlie Johnson of Pawhuska, Oklahoma, pulled their pistols and entered the bank's lobby while leaving a third unidentified man on the doorstep as a lookout. Sitting at his desk at the time was Lee Patrick, the bank's Vice President and standing at the main counter waiting on a customer (J. M. Reed) was Bookkeeper John Charles. According to statements

Stroud National Bank building now a legal office. Photo by Naomi Morgan.

made by the witnesses shortly after the robbery, Starr walked up to Charles throwing a white, flour sack on the counter demanding he "Open that safe and put the money in this bag." The bookkeeper filled the sack with roughly $1586 in both currency and silver. Spotting a second safe, Henry ordered the frightened accountant to open it; Charles replied it was on a time lock. The bandit, clearly agitated, began waving a big automatic in the air demanding, "Open it or I'll blow your damn head off." The bookkeeper told him "Don't you know what a time lock is? I can't open it."

Suddenly, Henry noticed a small girl stroll into the bank's lobby acting as though she hadn't a worry in the world. Starr demanded to know who the child belonged to. Patrick, still sitting at his desk, replied her name was Lorene Hughes, the daughter of a local businessman. Henry walked over to the child putting his hand on her head saying, "Run along little one." When the girl did not respond to his request, the bandit gave her a handful of coins telling her "Here, kiddie, go buy some ice cream." The young lass responded by taking the dough, but instead of leaving, she crawled up on a chair and sat there staring at the befuddled bandit. "Oh hell," exclaimed the outlaw, "She's balling up the works," adding, "Alright kid, stick around for the big show." Asking the bookkeeper if there was any more loot lying around, Charles pointed to a stack of dimes lying on the counter. Henry sneered saying "That's it?" Charles replied, "You've cleaned us out." With that said, Starr ordered the witnesses minus the little girl to walk out the back door. On reaching the alley, Henry noticed Patrick had a diamond stickpin stuck in his tie. Grabbing the little piece of jewelry, the outlaw exclaimed, "I know a gal who would like that." Patrick immediately began pleading with the bandit to return the item claiming it was a gift from his mother given to him shortly before her death. "Bullshit!" exclaimed Starr, "Partner, I've heard that mother story before, get moving." Prodding the three hostages through the alley, Starr stopped the party when it emerged on to the main street, instructing the group to, "Keep them hands down and do as I say or by G-d I'll kill ya."

After Lewis Estes and his three companions finished looting the First National Bank of roughly $4215, they emerged from the bank pushing a bevy of hostages in front of them. A few moments later, the two groups, plus their respective hostages, merged in the street and began moving toward their tethered horses located at the nearby stockyards.

Meanwhile, becoming aware of the ongoing robberies, the town's citizens began arming and taking up defensive positions. Suddenly, the vigilantes began peppering the fleeing outlaws with fire from a variety of firearms. Starr and Estes, bringing up the rear of the procession of bandits and hostages, answered their antagonists with several warning shots, one round nicking Charles Guild, a horse buyer. The bullet tore a hole in his coat and vest but otherwise did little damage. When a farmer named Walter Martin materialized across the street, Starr shouted at him to "Get back, you!" Martin glanced at the outlaw but then appeared to freeze in place. Henry again ordered him to "Get back!" When the farmer, who must have been petrified with fear didn't stir, Starr sent a .45 slug into his shoulder. The farmer suddenly found his sea legs, diving into an open doorway.

While the bandit was busy with the hapless spectator, twenty-year-old Paul Curry, armed with a 30.30 rifle he had taken from a shelf at a local butcher shop, situated himself behind an oaken barrel near his father's grocery store. Taking a bead on Starr as he attempted to mount his steed, the young man pulled the trigger. The bullet struck the bandit in the thigh ranging through his leg and breaking a bone as the missile followed its path of destruction. Henry hit the ground and lay temporarily paralyzed. The bold lad then sent a well aimed round into the neck of Lewis Estes, who although badly wounded and bleeding profusely, was able to mount his horse and flee the scene with the rest of the gang. Two carloads of officers and vigilantes following the bandit's trail found Estes leaning against a tree a couple of miles outside of town. When ordered to surrender he held a hand up meekly saying, "I'm played out." The wounded bandit was transported back to town where he joined Starr, who had been moved to a cot located in the office of Doctor John Evans. Three of the fleeing bank raiders, including Bud Maxfield, were captured the following month.

When Lee Patrick, the victimized Vice President of the Stroud National, visited the wounded bandits an hour after the raid, Starr informed him he could now have his diamond stickpin back. The outlaw also told the tending physician he could have his horse and saddle to pay for his medical bills. When the legendary bandit asked what the lad (Curry) had shot him with, he was told an old sawed-off hog-killing gun. Starr angrily responded, " Damn, not only shot by a mere boy, but a hog gun to boot."

That evening, when a crowd of rowdy citizens assembled and began making noises about holding a necktie party for the two wounded robbers, Starr

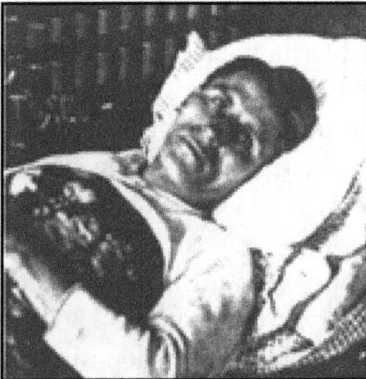

Henry Starr after being wounded in Stroud shootout. Courtesy Stroud Messenger.

Inside Stroud National Bank, John Charles, far left. Courtesy Stroud Messenger.

inquired of the doctor if he had any poison, saying "I don't mind dying, but I do fear being strung up." Later that evening Henry dictated a telegram to his mother stating "Come quick, I'm hurt bad." The following morning, photographer, C. T. Main convinced the grievously wounded bandit to have his picture taken. In the next edition of the local newspaper, "*The Stroud Messenger*," the wily businessman began advertising the sale of said photographs for ten cents each. It was reported he did a booming business for several weeks,

After Lewis Estes had recovered sufficiently from his wounds, he testified against his fellow bank raiders helping send several to long terms in the newly built Oklahoma State Penitentiary. Starr, realizing the hopelessness of his position, threw in the towel admitting his obvious guilt. Upon partially recovering from his injuries, the outlaw hobbled into court on crutches where he pled guilty to his participation in the robbery and was sentenced to a twenty-five-year stretch at McAlester. Due to his providing testimony against his comrades, Estes got off with only a five-year prison term. Paul Curry, the youth who had shot the pair of desperado's received a $1000 reward from the Oklahoma Banker's Association.

Amazingly, Starr, who throughout his colorful career had been the beneficiary of remarkable good public relations, was for a third time paroled after serving only four and a half years in prison. The dashing bandit, now forty-five-years-old, took up residence in Muskogee, Oklahoma for a short spell prior to moving to nearby Tulsa where he became involved with a motion picture company in filming his career in crime. The silent movie, dubbed the "Debtor to the Law," was based largely on the Stroud robbery. Although the film proved to have been well received and somewhat successful at the box office, it appears the bandit saw little of the profits come his way. The following year, Starr, who had by this time achieved considerable fame in the southwest United States, married an attractive twenty-three-year-old schoolteacher from Sallisaw, Oklahoma. The pair soon took up residence in Claremore, Oklahoma, where Henry spent his time taking the radium baths for his rheumatism and gambling in the local "sporting" houses. According to legendary lawmen Bud Ledbetter, "Henry was an easy mark for gamblers, he couldn't play poker very well and hated to be broke." Evidently, the outlaw had long been a gambleholic. His lack of luck with the pasteboards reportedly kept him in constant debt. In the days prior to the Harrison robbery, Starr was known

Deputy Federal Marshal Bud Ledbetter. Courtesy Okmulgee Public Library.

to have approached several area businessmen and lending institutions in an effort to borrow enough money to cover his gambling debts.

According to Oklahoma authorities, the bandit was last seen in Claremore on the day before the Harrison heist by Patrolman L. M. Rutherford eating breakfast with his wife at the Mecca Café at approximately 8 am. Lawmen suspected the bandit had disposed of the last of his ready cash the night before to a pair of professional gamblers at a local betting parlor.

Back at the Boone County, Arkansas, "Cross-Bar Hotel," a gravely wounded Henry Starr, was operated on. The attending physician, Doctor J. H. Fowler, reported the bandit's injuries would likely prove fatal; the offending projectile had not only severed his spinal column, but also destroyed a kidney. For the next few days, Starr slipped in and out of consciousness, constantly pleading for pain killing drugs. When awake, he ranged from one moment bragging about his prowess as a bandit to begging for the Lord's forgiveness for his wickedness. His young wife, sixteen-year-old son, and mother, being advised of his impending demise, soon arrived from Oklahoma, traveling through a snowstorm by rail. In conversations with his spouse and others, Starr claimed he had a premonition about the robbery, saying, "Something told me not to take the job, but I didn't want the others to think I was yellow." He also took full credit for saving the lives of the witnesses in the bank, saying, "I'm glad I ordered my accomplices to flee instead of fighting it out, Lord knows there would have been further bloodshed." "Balderdash!" replied Cashier Cleve Coffman when he was informed of the bandit's remarks. Adding, "His pals lit out on hearing the first shot, Starr didn't order them to flee nor did he save anyone's life."

Two days after the failed Harrison raid, a witness

from a recent bank robbery in Seligman, Missouri, appeared at the bandit's bedside positively identifying him as one of the perpetrators. According to news reports, the stickup had been a carbon copy of the Harrison job, minus the gunplay. The bank had reported a loss of $1232.23 and immediately posted a $400 reward for the capture of the robbers.

When questioned about the Seligman robbery, the outlaw strongly denied any involvement in the affair. When quizzed on the identities of his accomplices in the Harrison raid, the bandit asserted they were Buck Davis and Tom Jones. Boone County Sheriff J. Sibley Johnson scoffed at these pronouncements, telling the outlaw he was lying and urged him to come clean. Starr reportedly retorted, "If God directs I will share with you some valuable information." He must of received some divine guidance since the following morning the outlaw, realizing he was about to meet his maker, spilled the beans on his partners claiming he did so, hoping no innocent party would be blamed for the crime. For nearly an hour, he fessed up to a multitude of criminal acts as well as hinting he was

Dewey Cemetery. Courtesy of Naomi Morgan.

responsible for the December 20, 1920, Seligman bank robbery. The dying desperado also admitted the Harrison job had been planned in the Oklahoma town of Claremore, adding "I chose Harrison thinking no one would recognize me there, I was in debt and needed the money. I am sorry for my actions but the deed is done." He named his three partners as a pair of professional gamblers from Claremore and an acquaintance from nearby St. Joe, Arkansas. Later in the day, Oklahoma Governor J. B. A. Robertson, in an act many would characterize as "a day late and a dollar short," officially revoked Starr's parole.

At 1:25 Tuesday afternoon, Henry Starr, the so-called "Bandit King" of the Southwest died. His bullet-riddled body was prepared by a local undertaker and shipped by rail to Dewey, Oklahoma for burial. Two days later, Reverend J. B. Eldridge preached his funeral to the theme of "The thief who was forgiven on the cross," to a crowd of several hundred citizens assembled in and around the little Baptist church in Dewey. Ironically, the good reverend

Headline Boone County Headlight. Author's private collection.

also informed the crowd, the late desperadoes greatest quality had been loyalty to his friends. An odd statement, considering Starr's last living act was to snitch on his partners in the Harrison affair. The outlaw, who according to his mother had accepted Christ as his Savior in the hours before his death, was buried in the Dewey cemetery, his grave awash in colorful floral tributes.

Hearing the news of Starr's death, old time Oklahoma lawman Bill Tilghman commented, "Well, he always wished to die with his boots on, and heaven knows he took plenty of chances in order to make his wish come true." Adding, "Henry was a natural-born bank robber, but he may have been slipping; his last job wasn't well chosen nor were his partners."

Chapter 2

A Good Man Gone Bad

Meanwhile, back in Arkansas, lawmen were over-joyed with Starr's dramatic deathbed confession naming his partners in the aborted robbery. For the past four days, investigators had been running in circles tracking down useless clues such as a letter received by Banker W. J. Myers the day following the failed bank raid. The note, which was written in pencil and sent via the US mail, originated from the rail depot at Fort Smith, Arkansas. The writer of the correspondence assured the elderly Myers that revenge would be extracted upon his person for gunning down the famous bandit. After a brief inves-tigation, officers concluded the note was the work of a "nut."

As for the three individuals the legendary bandit named as his accomplices, the first was thirty-six-year-old Charlie Brackett, a longtime resident of Park Hill, Oklahoma. Orphaned at an early age, he was a product of the Cherokee Asylum. According to lawmen, the suspect had a reputation as a degenerate gambler who regularly haunted the betting parlors and horse racing tracks in Claremore, Muskogee, and Tulsa. On December 8, 1919, Charlie was charged with attempted murder in Cherokee County, Oklahoma. According to county court records, he had attacked and severely beaten a man named George Keys with a pair of oversized fence pliers. After his ar-rest, Brackett was incarcerated in the Cherokee County jail. On December 15, Justice of the Peace J. D. Wilson set his bond at $500 and bound his case over to the February 1920 term of the district court. Soon after his wife came up with the $500 for his freedom, Brackett jumped bond, preferring to go on the scout rather than face the music. Apparently, he packed up his spouse and small child fleeing to Claremore where he set up shop dealing poker at an illegal gambling den operated in the back room of a downtown pool hall.

The second man Starr fingered was twenty-nine-year-old Rufus Rollen who was born at Tahlequah, Cherokee Nation, but raised near Claremore, where he made a name for himself as a professional rodeo bronc rider in his youth. Rufus was well known to law enforcement circles as a shiftless character. He too, was an active enthusiast of the betting sports. Rollen was married with two children at the time of the investigation.

The final suspect, who allegedly drove the getaway car, was thirty-year-old David Edward Lockhart, known to his friends as simply "Ed." Although some census and prison reports note Lockhart as being born in the Indian Territory, modern day descendants claim his place of birth as Arkansas. His Father, a hard working dirt farmer, had immigrated to Searcy County, Arkansas with his family from Indiana shortly after the close of the Civil War. Two of Ed's uncles, Charley and Dave Lockhart, were noted area horse thieves. In September 1886, Charley was arrested and transported to the federal jail in Fort Smith, Arkansas on a charge of grand larceny (horse rustling). Due to a legal technicality, Judge Isaac C. Parker, to his great consternation, was forced to drop the pending charges and release the prisoner. A few weeks later, Charley and his brother raided a farm in Taney County, Missouri stealing a herd of hay burners. The owner of the ponies, along with a small posse, tracked the rustlers into Arkansas where they ambushed the pair killing Charley Lockhart at his sister's farm in Searcy County. Dave fled into the heavily timbered hills, but was captured and jailed at the nearby community of Eros. The following morning the outlaw escaped from the town's dilapidated jail. What became of him is unknown.

Raised near the present-day Ozark Mountain community of St. Joe, Arkansas, Ed, like most country boys of the era, was taught how to use a firearm as well as hunt and track wild game at an early age. He spent his youth wandering the surrounding wilderness, learning to move swiftly and silently through the thickly forested hills and hollows. While he received little formal education, (attending only four grades in school) he was noted as a clever, although mischievous lad.

In 1911, nineteen-year-old Ed moved with his father and stepmother (Lockhart's real mother died when he was three years old) to Oklahoma's Cookson Hills where he took a job as a farm hand. Soon afterward, he fell to cupid's arrow, marrying sixteen-year-old Alma Cherry. The couple moved into a clapboard farmhouse located near the crossroad settlement of Marble City. For the next few years, Lockhart kept his nose to the grindstone, sharecropping a small farm as well as cutting and hauling railroad ties for a living. During this time, the young couple was blessed with the birth of three children.

In early 1915, the ominous clouds of war were settling over the country. With the sinking of the British Liner Lusitania, which had 128 American civilians on board, the bloody world conflict being waged on the killing fields of the European continent was thrust upon America's shores. In April 1917, the United

Ed Lockhart .
Courtesy Muskogee Times- Democrat.

States declared war on the central powers of Germany, Austria-Hungary, and the Ottoman Empire. Young men began flooding the recruitment centers throughout the US filled with patriotic fever, anxious to defend the homeland. Even though Lockhart had a wife and children, he was no exception.

Shortly after America's entrance into the fray, he volunteered for duty. In early 1918, Ed joined the 36th "Lone Star" Division, made up of National Guard units from Texas and Oklahoma. After bidding his wife and family farewell, the twenty-seven-year-old recruit left home to begin his infantry training. On July 30, 1918, the division arrived in France a green untested fighting force. For the next few months, the 36th was involved in further training and joint maneuvers with French and British allied troops.

On September 26, a large French assault force slammed headlong into a German division occupying a position on the side of a precept named Blanc Mont (White Mountain), which was located on the German main line of resistance commonly known as the Hindenberg line. The French advance not only faltered but also turned into

RMS Lusitania. Author's private collection.

a general rout. Not wanting to cede precious ground, the French Generals begged U.S. Commanding General "Black Jack" Pershing to re-enforce their retreating forces in hopes of turning the tide. Pershing agreed, sending four battle tested regiments of Marines and the US 2nd Army Division to their relief. The American forces smashed into the enemy with such ferociousness as to send them reeling in retreat. After being pursued several miles, the Hun took up their previous positions on the mountain side. Pershing, not wanting to lose the momentum, attempted to force the enemy off their entrenched positions on and near the mountain top. As insurance of success, the iron willed American Commander added the unblooded 36th into the fray. The battle for Mont Blanc raged for over two weeks before the German force, faced with enormous losses, bolted down the mountain side in full retreat not stopping until they found sanctuary at a stopgap line of trenches and pillboxes which had been hastily set up and re-enforced by the German high command. The vicious little struggle turned out to be one of America's costliest victories in the First World War, with U.S. units suffering over 6,300 casualties.

Thick in the midst of this violent nightmare was Ed Lockhart and another Sequoyah County man named Charlie Price, who we will hear more of as the story proceeds. From all reports, Lockhart not only came through the battle unscathed but was also decorated for bravery. Records indicate he was a splendid soldier and had done his folks back home proud. The 36th went on to participate in the massive Muese-Argonne offensive, which broke the enemies back, thus ending the war. Following the November 11, 1918, German surrender, America began the process of transporting the more than two million doughboys back home using a fleet of cannibalized luxury

American troops in France WWI. Author's private collection.

liners and troopships. In early 1919, Ed Lockhart and his comrades in the "Lone Star" Division firmly placed their feet back on US soil.

According to news reports, descendants, and old-timers, the war changed Lockhart for the worse. The old saying "once they've seen gay Paree, there's no getting 'em back on the farm" was certainly applicable in his case. Leaving for war a hardworking farmer and dedicated family man, he returned a restless shadow of his former self. Soon after his homecoming to Marble City, the ex-doughboy not only "took to the bottle," but also acquired the gambling habit, betting on the ponies at illegal racing events (pari-mutuel racing was banned in Oklahoma from 1915 to 1982), and sitting in on round-the-clock poker and dice games.

Around this time, Lockhart became involved with a neighboring family named Dotson, who were renown for their wild and raucous ways. The leaders of the Dotson clan appear to have been forty-year-old Berry and his brother Abe. The brothers were a pair of tough, unruly mountain men who had a passion for home made whiskey and an immense hatred for the forces of law and order. Two of Berry's three sons, Lewis (Bee) and Charley, would evolve into arch-criminals of the worse stripe under their old man's tutelage, while the third sibling seems to have taken no part in his brothers' sordid activities.

Another of Lockhart's "good-time buddies" appears to have been his ex-comrade in arms, Charlie Price, a fellow veteran of the "Lone Star" Division, who was the son of an early day pioneer who the nearby community of Prices Chapel was named. Charlie, who was widely noted in his youth as "full of piss and vinegar," was the fourth of five brothers. The eldest, Reece, was also a veteran of the "Great War." He was apparently an ingenious fellow who had invented several safety devises for the railroad. Although often described as quiet and unassuming, he was known as the "bell cow" amongst the brothers. Next in age was Mack, followed by George, who lived near the small hill settlement of Cookson, Oklahoma. William, nicknamed "Tump" was the youngest born in 1897. The boys were distantly related through their mother's lineage to Henry Starr. The lives of four of these

Horseplay with the Dotsons, Marble City, Oklahoma.
Courtesy Dr. Mark Dotson.

five siblings will later intrude violently into this narrative.

Within a year of the war's end, Lockhart's wife called it quits, abandoning the wild young man to his evil devices. A few months later, she filed for divorce. Ed drifted back to Searcy County, Arkansas where two of his brothers still resided. He soon discovered other female companionship and by early 1919 had remarried to nineteen-year-old Mara "Maude" Sitton. After stashing his pregnant wife in a rented house in Harrison, Arkansas, the newlywed began traveling the area's well-known gambling circuit with his spirited younger brother Sam, betting on the ponies and trying his hand in high-stakes poker games in Tulsa and Claremore, Oklahoma. While visiting the latter location, the ex-war hero sought out fellow gamblers, Charley Brackett and Rufus Rollen. What motivated this trio of drifters to make the career switch from gambling to bank robbery is unknown, but the most likely scenario suggests Lockhart lured his newfound friends into assisting him in a scheme to rob his hometown bank. Not knowing the first thing about knocking over banks, the group subsequently recruited the services of the legendary and always cash-poor Henry Starr, who was known to have frequently played poker with Charlie Brackett.

The first big break in the manhunt for the remaining Harrison bank robbery suspects came only a few days after the dying Henry Starr's confession, when Rogers County officers, assisted by members of the Craig County Sheriff's department, began shadowing the wife of Rufus Rollen in Claremore, Oklahoma. Lawmen were convinced the suspect's better half would lead them to the fugitive's whereabouts. They also believed she would eventually arrange a meeting with the desperado in Muskogee where his mother and brother resided. On the morning of the February 24th, Mrs. Rollen was observed delivering her two children, who were later discovered to be suffering from a case of the measles, to the care of a relative. She then boarded a southbound passenger train. Close on her heels were Deputy Sheriffs E. D. Ridenhour and Jesse Tartar who also boarded the train. Craig County Sheriff H. E. Ridenhour wired ahead to Muskogee County Sheriff Jim Robbins informing him of her movements. Several hours later, Muskogee Deputy Sheriffs W. O. Manly and Mont Grady spotted the subject dismounting the train at Muskogee's KATY Depot. The Muskogee lawmen quickly connected with their fellow officers from the train and continued to shadow the woman. Within the hour, Mrs. Rollen was observed entering the home of her brother-in-law on the city's east side. The officers settled down to a stakeout watching the residence until nearly midnight when they observed a lone figure resembling the description of the fugitive stroll on to the front porch. When the two Muskogee deputies approached the man, he fled into the house down a long hallway and leaped through a screened window located at the rear of the dwelling. Unfortunately for him, he fell directly into the waiting arms of the Craig County lawmen. Knowing he was bested, the fugitive promptly surrendered without a struggle.

After being lodged in the Muskogee County jail for several days where he at first denied any involvement in the Harrison robbery, the prisoner finally caved in, confessing his part in the raid. The following morning, Sheriff Johnson of Boone County, Arkansas showed up at the jail with extradition papers in hand.

On arrival in Harrison, the fugitive, who was suffering from several days of vigorous questioning and probably a healthy dose of physical abuse, willingly pled guilty before the District Judge and was given a sentence of three years hard labor at the notorious Tucker Prison Farm.

According to Arkansas authorities, Rollen confessed not only his part in the crime, but like his deceased comrade, Henry Starr, spilled the beans on everyone involved.

In the mean time, Rollen's ex-partners, Ed Lockhart and Charlie Brackett, sought sanctuary in the infamous Cookson Hills area of Eastern Oklahoma. Lockhart, who had lived over a decade in the hills near Marble City, reportedly knew every creek, hollow, hill, cave, and wild game trail in the district. He was also familiar with a great many residents, especially the shady ones. For the next few months, the pair spent their time sampling the local moonshine and strutting their stuff at every barn dance in a three-county area. Lawmen also suspected the duo of participating in several horse-theft raids across the border into Arkansas during their sojourn in the hills.

Sheriff H. E. Ridenhour. Courtesy Claremore Progress.

Chapter Three

A Cast of Dubious Characters

Although Oklahoma's Cookson Hills was a place long branded as the headquarters of evildoers and blood-thirsty desperadoes, in reality the isolated and heavily-forested hills were populated by far more churchgoers than outlaws. While the region had contributed its' fair share of bad men to society, many of the outlaws in residence were outsiders who had immigrated there due to the district's inaccessible nature and long-standing reputation as a bandit's rendezvous.

One of Lockhart and Brackett's favorite places of refuge was a small general merchandise store located in the backwater Cookson Hills settlement of Barber, which was owned by a character dubbed "Cotton Top" Walker, so named for the small whiff of thin blond hair remaining on his otherwise bald head. Walker's store offered not just asylum from law, but a jug, a hot deck of cards, and a host who never stopped trying to figure a way to make a dishonest buck. Conspiracy was always in the air.

Indeed, Fredrick L. Walker Sr. was known far and wide for his wheedling, devious ways. Cursed with the

Fred Walker. Courtesy Muskogee Times-Democrat.

Modern day view of the old Barber store, since renovated into a residence, but now abandoned. Photo by Naomi Morgan.

morals of an alley cat, he considered the law just another obstacle to making an easy living. Although most outsiders who made his acquaintance usually regretted the experience, many of his neighbors held genuine affection for the pudgy "flimflam man." Born in the Indian Territory in the 1876, Walker was 20 percent Cherokee and 100 percent crook. He was described as short, squat, nervous, and talkative. Blessed with a keen intellect and a usually jolly disposition, he reportedly had the ability to

Foundation ruins of original site of the store, moved to higher ground from this flood plane created by the construction of Ten Killer Lake.

STATE OF OKLAHOMA,
CHEROKEE COUNTY

THE STATE OF OKLAHOMA,
                    Plaintiff,   IN DISTRICT COURT.
         vs

...........Fred Walker,........... No.................

....
                    Defendant.

IN THE NAME AND BY THE AUTHORITY OF THE STATE OF OKLAHOMA.
At the..September,...............19.09.Term of the District Court of Cherokee County,
State of Oklahoma, begun and held at the City of Tahlequah in said County on the.....7th.........
day of..September,Nineteen Hundred and..9. the Grand Jury of said County, good and lawful
men, legally drawn and Summoned according to law, and then and there examined, impaneled,
sworn and charged according to law, to diligently inquire into, and true presentment make, of all
public offenses against the State of Oklahoma, committed or triable within said County, upon their
said oaths, in the name and by the authority of the State of Oklahoma, do present and find that the
said.........Fred Walker,...Cherokee County, and State of Oklahoma,
on the...20th..........day of....August,.............in the year of our Lord One Thousand
Nine Hundred and .nine,. ....and prior to the finding of this indictment
.....................................did ,. in said County and State, on or about
the 20th day of August ,1909, unlawfully and willfully, sell one
pint of spirituous liquor, one pint of vinous liquor, one pint
fermented liquor, one pint of malt liquor, to W. H. Winder, for
the sum of Twenty cents,

contrary to the form of the statutes in such cases made and provided, and against the peace and
dignity of the State.
                            ....J. J. Conway.............
                            County Attorney in and for said County

*One of Fred Walker's many bootlegging charges. Courtesy
Cherokee County Court Clerk.*

talk a man out of his last nickel. On most days, he could be found holding court in front of either a checkerboard or a fast game of cards (he had a weakness for stud poker) next to a pot bellied stove located in the center of the store, which was operated by him and his kin. Nipping on a crock jug of his own home made whiskey and making good use of a conveniently located spittoon, the likable rogue would spin his web of bullshit till it damn near smothered all those in attendance.

According to Cherokee County court records, Walker was arrested thirty times in the first two decades of the twentieth century on charges ranging from transporting ardent spirits to horse and auto theft. (Actually, he was charged but not formally arrested with another seventy whiskey violations between 1898-1922) Apart from the time he was sentenced to a short jolt in Leavenworth, he was able to wiggle out of his troubles without enduring serious consequences.

In 1909, Walker was briefly jailed for selling a neighbor's farm twice in one week to visiting "Greenhorns." The neighbor, who had unfortunately chosen that week to visit an ailing relative in Arkansas, was none the wiser. When the gullible buyers complained, the County Judge threw the energetic swindler in the clink for a few weeks before releasing him upon his reimbursing his unlucky customers most of their down payments. The following year, he and a pal were incarcerated for the theft of a herd of hogs. Apparently, they weaseled out of the charges by paying a small fine and returning the porkers to their rightful owners. As for his family, Walker was married to a respectable schoolteacher, who was cursed with only a single fault, bad taste in husbands. Of his five children, one daughter was married to a local hellion named Curtis "Ed" Hays and another to Mack Moore. Tragically, Walker's youngest son was crippled from a fall off a horse at the age of twelve.

Although the middle-aged miscreant once acted as a Deputy for the famous Revenuer "Pussyfoot" Johnson for a short period, (Johnson fired him) he was also a well-known whiskey maker. Many old-timers say, after the legendary Silas Fountain he was the finest manufacturer of "Wildcat" in the hills. This was a bold statement, considering Federal Marshal Joe Wilson once claimed there were more whiskey stills on the Illinois River per square mile than in the mountains of Kentucky. Evidently, Walker peddled his potent product out of his little General Store in Barber and his cabin on nearby Dry Creek.

The most amazing thing about "Cotton" was the fact in 1918 he was somehow elected or appointed a Justice of the Peace for the Barber area. It's been told he dispensed justice according to how much corn liquor he had consumed that day or the size of the bribe. The larcenous storekeeper was also the Postmaster at Barber for several years. Over time, old "Cotton Top" became the "Big Dog" in the Barber area.

While "scouting" in the Cooksons, Lockhart and Brackett also fell in with a pair of Walker's running buddies. The first was an elderly vagabond dubbed "Kaiser Bill" Goodman, so named for his habit of sporting a long handlebar mustache similar to Germany's Kaiser Wilhelm's. Goodman, like his pal Walker, was a man of dubious character. According to local legend, "Kaiser," began his career in crime with a train robbery on the plains of Kansas in the 1880s. The old man claimed to have once ridden with the infamous Dalton Gang. One thing is for sure; he operated under more names than Elizabeth Taylor. Although he was most often referred to as John R. Goodman, his true name was never documented. Prison records indicate he was born in the 1850s, somewhere in Pennsylvania. Rumor has it he immigrated west in the

Prison photo of the notorious "Kaiser Bill," minus his famous whiskers, circa 1925. Courtesy Muskogee Phoenix.

1870s running from a murder charge. He soon joined the US Calvary at Fort Sill, located in the then Indian Territory, under the name G. S. White, and may have participated in the Red River Indian War. Within a year of his enlistment, he walked away from his military commitment and was branded a deserter

In the 1880s and '90s Goodman gambled, drank, and robbed his way through the Indian Territory and Kansas. According to reports published years later, he was a suspect in several small store robberies as well as both a bank and train robbery during this time. In 1901, he was arrested and convicted of distributing ardent spirits to the Indians and sentenced to Leavenworth Penitentiary, under the name of Hale. It was believed he might have first made the acquaintance of "Cotton" Walker during his stay there. Shortly after his parole, he was convicted of horse theft in Missouri.

In 1906, he served a term at the Arkansas State Pen for armed robbery using the name John G. Smith. It was a year into his term before prison officials concluded Smith was not his true name. After an investigation and a great deal of prodding, the fifty-some-year-old outlaw admitted his legal name was Charlie O'Dell (also a lie). Sometime after his release around 1910, the doddering bandit drifted into the thug infested Cookson Hills where he hooked-up with the likes of "Cotton" Walker.

One bizarre story about "Kaiser" which dates from early 1918 involves the time he strolled into the Central

STATE OF OKLAHOMA,
Cherokee County. } ss.

BEFORE......................J. D. Wilson...
                                                                    Justice of the Peace

In and for Cherokee County, State of Oklahoma, comes.......................S. M. Redburn.........................

and makes complaint on oath and says that on or about the 16th day of......April....A. D. 1918,

at and within said County of Cherokee and State of Oklahoma, one ......John R. Goodman.........................

....did then and there unlawfully ....

commit the crime of obtaining money by false pretenses in the manner and form as follows, to-wit:

That is to say, the said John R. Goodman did, in Cherokee County, State of Oklahoma, and on or about the 16th day of April, 1918, then and there being, then and there, unlawfully, designedly, fraudulently and feloniously obtain from the Central National Bank, a corporation of Tahlequah, Oklahoma, the sum of $317.00, in good and lawfuly money of the United States of America, of the value of $317.00, by then and there falsely, designedly, fraudulently and feloniously representing to said Central National Bank that he, the said John R. Goodman, was then and there the owner of fifteen yearling heifers, and five two year old heifers, branded JJbar on left side; five yearling heifers and five cows, ranging from three to five years of age, branded JR connected on left side and G on left hip, and three calves, no marks or brands, and by then and there executing a chattel mortgage to said Central National Bank, covering the property herein described, to secure the payment of said sum of $317.00, so received by said John R. Goodman, from said Central National Bank, when in truth and in fact he, the said John R. Goodman, was not the owner of the property herein described as he, the said John R. Goodman, then and there well knew; but the said Central National Bank, relying on the representations of the said John R. Goodman that he was the owner of said property, and believing said representations to be true was induced to and did loan to said John R. Goodman the sum of $317.00 as aforesaid, which said representations on the part of the said John R. Goodman were then and there made with intent to cheat, wrong, and defraud said Central National Bank out of said sum of $317.00, as aforesaid,

Contrary to the form of the Statute in such case made and provided, and against the peace and dignity of the State of Oklahoma.

Wherefore,......he prays that a warrant may issue for the arrest of the said.....John R. Goodman..................

....that......he may be dealt with according to law.

S. M. Redburn

Sworn and subscribed to before me this......29th......day of......July......................, 1918,

J. D. Wilson
                                                                    Justice of the Peace.

Warrant for Goodman on a fraud-larceny charge 1918- Cherokee County, Oklahoma. Courtesy Cherokee County Court Clerk.

National Bank of Tahlequah taking out loans for $300 and $317 respectively using the name John R. Goodman. Evidently, the outlaw (who was probably working in concert with Fred Walker at the time) gained the loans by using a herd of cattle and a small farm located near Cookson as collateral. Problem was, the old thief didn't own said cattle or land. After the notes were several months overdue, the financial institution sent an emissary into the hills in search of their money. When the collector inquired of the locals if they knew a man by the name of John Goodman, they broke into laughter. Realizing they had been hustled, the bank promptly filed fraud and theft charges against the bandit. Needless to say, the bank never saw their $617 come home to roost.

Young Mount Cookson. Courtesy Daily Democrat, Fayetteville, Arkansas.

Another of Walker's cronies Lockhart connected with was a large, wide shouldered, muscular fellow with bushy eyebrows named Levi Mount Cookson. At thirty-three-years of age, "Mount," as he was called, was an enigma. Born into one of the great prosperous pioneer families of Eastern Oklahoma (his Uncle was the namesake of the hills) who were generally known for their honest, law abiding ways; he eventually evolved into one of the most celebrated outlaws to ever come out of the Cookson Hills.

On the morning of September 8, 1918, Walker, and his two comrades saddled their horses and began riding south in search of some "easy money." After journeying some thirty miles to the small Sequoyah County community of Gore, the trio dismounted in front of the Farmers State Bank of Illinois. "Cotton" Walker held the horses while "Kaiser" and Mount Cookson entered the institution with guns drawn. The bank's chief cashier, Bruce Foreman, was chatting with an Indian acquaintance about the price of cotton when he noticed two rough looking men wearing long slickers and donning "cowboy" hats lumber into the lobby, one carrying a long-barreled pistol and the other, an older man (later known to have been "Kaiser Bill") toting a sawed off double barrel shotgun. According to a statement Foreman later made to police, the elderly fellow, who struck him as mean in appearance, looked him square in the eye and said with a loud voice, "Put 'em up, Buster." The younger man, (Mount Cookson) who the cashier stated had bushy eyebrows, then dashed behind the counter cleaning out the tills to the tune of $3076 in cash and coin. The pair evidently did not attempt to enter the locked vault that held another $4000. On backing out the front door, the older man ordered the witnesses to "Come outside with us." On reaching the sidewalk he ordered them to "Stay put and don't move a muscle." Luckily for the bandits, the street was empty due to it being dinnertime. Foreman then observed another man (Walker) who he described as squat and bald in appearance but wearing a bandana over his face, meet

Bank of Illinois at Gore, Oklahoma, circa 1920.
Courtesy Paul Eichling.

the pair with three horses, one described as a big bay and the others as grays. Two of the bandits then rode out of town in cloud a of dust, while the older man with the shotgun riding the bay, slowly backed his horse towards the edge of town, while holding his "street sweeper" at the ready. On the perimeter of the village, the robber discharged one barrel of the shotgun in the air and let out a whoop before spurring his horse towards freedom.

Within minutes of the raid, the alarm went out throughout the countryside. Armed posses from the nearby communities of Webbers Falls and Vian began converging on the scene driving Model "T" automobiles and mounted on horses and mules. After organizing into two large groups, the vigilantes struck north following the bandits' trail. The offices of Muskogee County Sheriff John Barger as well as Sequoyah County Sheriff C. M. "Goodlow" Gay were notified and both promptly sent teams of officers heading into the district. During the afternoon, the vigilantes struck the robbers' trail near Tenkiller Ferry but soon lost sight of it due to the bandit's clever tactic of crossing and recrossing the Illinois River. After following the waterway for several hours, the fugitives struck inland to the east. Near the village of Box, a local Indian joined the posse contributing a pack of bloodhounds to the effort. Apparently, the bandits had prepared

Muskogee County Sheriff John Barger. Courtesy Three Rivers Museum and Muskogee County Sheriff's Department.

for this eventuality. They reacted by pouring the contents of several bags of red pepper on their track. When the sensitive noses of the high powered hounds hit the pepper dosed trail the dogs were promptly turned from sophisticated tracking machines to common pot-lickers.

That evening, the Gore posse made contact with the fleeing desperadoes just north of Marble City, located on the southern edge of the Cookson Hills. A few shots were exchanged but none took effect. As dusk turned to dark, the Gore group now joined by officers from Muskogee and Sallisaw surrounded a large thicket where the outlaws were suspected to have taken refuge. Figuring they had their prey securely hemmed in, Sheriff Gay made the decision to wait for daybreak and re-enforcements before rushing the tract of brambles, due to his fear the posse would become confused in the darkness and possibly shoot one another. The following morning, the party of lawmen made their way into the thicket only to be met by a few rabbits and a pair of deer. The fugitives had given them the slip under the cover of darkness.

A few days after the robbery the bulk of the posse gave up the chase, disbanded and went home. On the ride back to town, one of the vigilantes named W. R. Breedlove of Gore spotted a green bundle lying by the roadside. On closer inspection, the bundle turned out to be a packet containing $500 in assorted denominations. The thick package was wrapped in paper, which read, "Property of the Farmers Bank of Illinois, Gore, Oklahoma." Breedlove, obviously the honest type, promptly turned over the cash to the bank, while loudly suggesting the loot had "Shaken out of the bandit's pockets while performing their hard ride to freedom."

Within days of the heist, the Gore Bank was back in business. The president of the institution claimed the missing loot was fully insured and publicly swore, "These robbers represent no more than a minor nuisance." He further stated, "No bandit could do serious harm to the soundness of this institution." He would live to regret these bold statements. The bank soon posted a $500 reward for the capture of the brigands who had ravaged their business.

Little headway was made towards the solving of the crime until the morning of October 6, 1918, when Sheriff Gay received intelligence from an informant who was obviously hoping to collect a piece of reward money. His information concerned a mysterious character named "Dad" Smith, who hung out around the Cookson Hill settlements of Barber and Cookson. According to the stool pigeon, "Dad" and his pals Mount Cookson and "Cotton" Walker had recently made a big haul and were all three flush with ready cash, which was a rare occurrence in the poverty ridden district. On contacting Cherokee County authorities, Gay was informed that Walker and Cookson were known scoundrels, both men having lengthy records of bad behavior in the past. Officials there also responded they were aware of the presence in their county of the infamous "Dad" Smith, alias John R. "Kaiser" Goodman. Although local law enforcement officers had not actually set eyes on the shadowy figure, the Cherokee County Sheriff's Department did hold a pair of arrest warrants for him on charges of lar-

Sequoyah County Sheriff C.M. Gay. Courtesy Sequoyah County Sheriff's Department.

ceny-fraud. They agreed to meet Gay and a party of officers, which included Federal Marshal Joe Wilson and a pair of Pinkerton detectives, hired by the bank's insurance company, at a point just south of the village of Barber.

At dawn, October 7, 1918, five officers raided the home of Mount Cookson, capturing the stocky outlaw in his bed. Found sleeping in an outbuilding was an elderly gentleman, whom lawmen claimed had to be restrained from grabbing an old-fashioned horse pistol lying on a nearby bench. Although the old man identified himself as Ernest Gregg, Cookson's hired hand, lawmen suspected he was in reality the notorious "Kaiser Bill." At nearly the same time as the raid was taking place at Cookson's residence, five other minions of the law swooped down on "Cotton" Walker's ramshackle residence near Barber. According to news reports, "Cotton" gave up peacefully but his wife became hysterical demanding the immediate release of her husband. Only small sums of money were found at either home. The trio of suspects were handcuffed and transported by Model "T" Touring car to Sallisaw where they were lodged in the county jail. When the cashier, Bruce Foreman, positively identified both "Kaiser" and Cookson as being two of the three individuals who had held up the bank, the suspects were officially charged with armed robbery and bound over for trial. Charges were grudgingly dropped against Walker when Foreman failed to positively identify him as the masked man who held his companion's horses outside the bank.

The trial of Mount Cookson was reportedly a spirited affair. Although his attorney, W. J. Crump of Muskogee put up a game fight, a jury of his peers found him guilty. The following day, Judge Arnold sentenced the defendant to a term of five years in the state rock pile. Cookson immediately posted a $5000 bond, enabling him to gain his temporary freedom until the State Court of Appeals could hear his case. On December 10, "Kaiser Bill," now claiming his true name was not Ernest Gregg but Rufus Battle came to trial. According to news reports, the hard-boiled bandit sat silently gnawing on a chaw of tobacco throughout the three-day trial. "Kaiser" refused to testify in his defense and when asked his plea, he reportedly sent a stream of tobacco juice flying towards the docket with some of the spittle spattering the bailiff's shiny shoes. The outlaw, who his jailors described as "A crotchety old bastard," was found guilty and promptly sentenced to fifteen years in record time. When the Judge inquired if the picturesque rogue had any final remarks he wanted to share with the court, the elderly gentleman instructed his honor to "Kiss his ass" in open court. The frazzled jurist ordered the unruly defendant physically removed from the courtroom.

After sentencing, "Kaiser" was apparently not a happy camper. In the days following his conviction, the colorful if not very hygienic desperado assaulted a fellow inmate, chewing off half his right ear before the guards subdued him. The surly bandit claimed the man had

Sequoyah County courthouse and jail. Courtesy Sequoyah County Historical Society.

"sorely" insulted him. The following day, the old outlaw banged a guard over the head with a full chamber pot when the officer had the audacity to ask him if he was ready for supper. After spending several days in the cooler, the old boy was overheard telling a fellow inmate he was planning on dropping a dime on his coconspirators if they didn't find a way to get him out of his current bind, claiming he wasn't going to "take the fall" for anyone.

In the early morning hours of December 21, the night jailor heard a loud rap on the heavy main door. When the jailor, who had been enjoying a short snooze, inquired who was knocking, a voice responded, saying it was Mose Newman (the Sallisaw city night cop) with a prisoner. When the keeper opened the door, he was greeted with a gun barrel leveled at his chest. Two masked men forced their way into the jail's confines relieving the officer of his keys. One of the men, described as stocky, walked directly to "Kaiser's" cell. On unlocking the barred door, Goodman and his cell mate Will Nix, who was being held on a grand larceny charge, walked briskly towards the bastille's exit stopping just long enough for "Kaiser" to give the jailor a firm kick in the backside and a good cussing. The younger, stocky-built individual then locked the hapless warden in "Kaiser's" now vacant cell. Before departing the jailhouse, the quartet looted the prison's armory of a dozen rifles and shotguns. After an hour of screaming at the top of his lungs, the poor jailor was discovered imprisoned in his own prison by a store owner who lived nearby. A posse was formed and scoured the area for several days seeking the fugitive's whereabouts, but drew a blank.

Within a week of the bold jail delivery, Will Nix, Goodman's ex-cell mate and fellow escapee was captured in Texas. After some intense prodding, the prisoner spilled his guts giving the names of his coconspirators. He informed lawmen the crew of jail raiders was made up of "Cotton" Walker, his sidekick Mount Cookson, and an unnamed individual, which authorities suspected was Marble City's own Berry Dotson. An angry Sheriff Gay, joined by a group of Cherokee and Muskogee County officers, swiftly swooped down on the residences of Walker and Cookson arresting and charging the pair with the jail break. They also arrested a relative of Cookson who tried to alibi the outlaw on the night of the escape, charging him with obstruction of justice. After conducting a lengthy search, authorities failed to uncover the present whereabouts of Dotson. The trio of prisoners was hauled to Muskogee where they were lodged in the county jail, which lawmen considered more secure than the Sallisaw facility, pending disposition of the charges.

Unluckily for the officers, when their star witness, Will Nix, was called in front of the grand jury, his testimony fell apart under cross examination, resulting in the prompt release of the three suspects, although Cookson remained on appeal bond for his part in the Gore bank heist. The prosecuting attorney, cursing his luck, was reportedly in a state of nervous exhaustion over the case.

One year later on December 16, 1919, two masked men, one wearing a large sombrero and both donning full-length army overcoats, rode horseback up to the front entrance of the Citizens State Bank of Gans, Oklahoma. After tying their horses, one a bay and the other a gray, to an iron pipe that acted as a hitching post, the pair was observed strolling unhurriedly into the financial institution. According to a statement given by Cashier Frank Hopper, who was standing behind the counter talking to two customers at the time, "Two men, one much older than the other, walked up to me with pistols drawn." The old man bellowed to "Stand and Deliver," The trio of witnesses were then ordered to lie on the floor while the

Gans, Oklahoma today. Photo by Naomi Morgan.

younger bandit rifled the tills and vault, whilst the elderly fellow covered the bystanders with a big horse pistol. After collecting nearly $3000 in cash and coin, the robbers locked the three in the vault and dashed toward their horses.

Unfortunately for the robbers, the bank's chief cashier, E. C. Gilbert, returning to work from a local eatery, observed the thieves making their getaway. Gilbert responded by running into a nearby hardware store where he requested the owner and several customers to assist him in thwarting the bandits. After arming himself and the others with large caliber repeating rifles taken from the stores shelves, Gilbert and party dashed into the road ready for action.

By the time the gutsy cashier and his comrades hit the street the robbers were nearly one hundred yards down the town's main road spurring their mounts into a brisk gait towards freedom. Gilbert, raising a rifle to his shoulder, took careful aim firing three shots in rapid succession. Witnesses standing nearby noticed the last shot struck pay dirt. The younger of the outlaws flinched and flung headfirst into the street, dropping the flour sack containing the loot. His elderly companion, in a rage of profanity, returned fire while at the same time pulling his partner back into his saddle. Taking the reins of both horses, he began flogging their rumps with a loud slap of leather.

The fleeing horsemen quickly disappeared into a nearby patch of timber in a cloud of dust and the sound of clattering hooves.

Gilbert, now joined by a dozen armed citizens, ran to the point where the bandit had fell into the road. They quickly discovered a blood soaked sack of money, which the highwaymen in their hurried escape had failed to retrieve. On lifting the stolen loot, the posse quickly realized why the robbers had appeared to struggle with the bag. It was filled with not only paper money, but nearly 400 silver dollars as well. Within minutes of the robbery, a hastily assembled group of over fifty men riding horses and driving automobiles began following the outlaw's trail. They were soon joined by a group of officers headed by Sequoyah County Sheriff B. F. Faulkner. With the onset of darkness, the posse lost sight of the fugitive's tracks near the base of Wildhorse Mountain south of Sallisaw. The following day, several alert citizens came forward claiming they had seen the pair of bandits riding through Sallisaw heading east toward Gans the night before the robbery.

B. F. Faulkner. Courtesy Sequoyah County Sheriff's Department.

The following day Sequoyah County officers informed an assembled crowd of reporters, they suspected the participants in the raid were "Kaiser Bill" Goodman and thirty-six-year-old Bushyhead "Bush" Wood, a known "tough," who was also a suspect in several area burglaries. According to

FORM 150.

INDICTMENT FOR MURDER IN THE INDIAN TERRITORY.

(U. S. Attorney's Office No. ....)

(Grand Jury No. ....)

Court No. ....

United States of America,)
INDIAN TERRITORY, } ss.
Northern .... District.)

In the United States Court in the Indian Territory, for the _Northern_ District
of said Territory, at the _October_ Term, A. D. ~~189~~ 1907
at Vinita

UNITED STATES
versus
Bush Woods)

) INDICTMENT FOR MURDER.

Defendant .)

The Grand Jurors of the United States of America, duly selected, summoned, impaneled, sworn, and
charged to inquire within and for the body of the _Northern_ District of the Indian Territory
aforesaid, in the name and by the authority of the United States, upon their oaths do find, present, and
charge that one _Bush Woods_

...., on the _21st_ day of
June , A. D. ~~189~~ 1907, within the _Northern_ District of the Indian Territory
aforesaid, with force and arms, in and upon the body of one _Thomas Townsend_
then and there being, feloniously, willfully, and of _his_ malice aforethought, did make an assault;
and that the said _Bush Woods_

with a certain _gun_
then and there charged with gunpowder and one leaden bullet, which said _gun_ he the said
Bush Woods

in _his_ hand then and there had and held, then and there feloniously, willfully, and of _his_ malice
aforethought, did discharge and shoot off, at, to, against, and upon the body of the said ....
Thomas Townsend , and that the said
Bush Woods

Bush Wood indictment on a murder charge. Courtesy Cherokee County Court Clerk.

Sheriff's officials, Wood, who came from a respected Cherokee County family, was a man with a checkered past. His first serious brush with the law occurred in 1903, when he was arrested in Cherokee County for carrying a concealed weapon. In 1907, he shot and killed a man named Thomas Townsend in a drunken brawl at a barn dance near Tahlequah, Oklahoma. When tried in Federal court, the Judge reduced the charge to aggravated assault and sentenced Wood to a year in jail along with a hefty fine. Following his marriage in 1909, it appears he spent the next half-dozen years living the life of a sober and industrious dirt farmer. He apparently "went native," drinking heavily and falling in with bad company after the unfortunate death of his young wife in 1916.

Area lawmen openly speculated the pair of bandits had likely been aided and abetted in the bank raid by none other than "Cotton" Walker in both the planning of the robbery and their subsequent escape from justice.

In the fall of 1920, the same duo strolled into the Farmers Bank of Gore relieving the institution of over $2000. The pair was described by one of the witnesses as a real "Odd-ball" team. One bandit, who appeared "getting on in years," was calm and professional, while the other man was young and fidgety, waving his pistol around in a careless manner while hurling threats of bodily harm toward the gathered witnesses.

Chapter 4

Bold Lads in Search of Easy Money

At 1:30 on the afternoon of April 25, 1921, three individuals in a rusted out Ford car parked in front of the First State Bank of Locust Grove, Oklahoma. Two of the men hurriedly slipped on masks that partially covered their faces before strolling towards the building's main door while a third remained in the running automobile. On entering the bank's lobby, one of the men ordered Assistant Cashier M. K. Hatfield and Bookkeeper Gertrude Suggs, to "Get them hands in the air!" The robbers then scooped up $2,200 in cash as well as $2,750 in negotiable Liberty Bonds, which they stuffed in both a leather satchel and a feed sack. When the bandits started for the door intent on making their getaway, they spotted H. B. Hanson, the owner of a nearby hardware store, standing in the street next to the bank holding a .22 caliber rifle in his hands. Turning toward the pair of witnesses the lead robber stated, "It looks like there's going to be trouble, you two best get in the vault so you don't get killed."

Within minutes of the robbery's completion, the two employees released themselves from the vault by undoing a setscrew from the locking mechanism. On reaching the bank's lobby, the witnesses dived for cover when they heard what sounded like several gun blasts. After lying on the marble floor for several minutes waiting for the danger to pass, the victims made their way to the street where the store owner, still toting his rifle greeted them. Thinking Hanson had engaged the robbers in a gun battle, they inquired if he had gotten the villains. He replied with a straight face, "Yes, several of them." When the bank employees began happily slapping him on the shoulders, he asked if they were always so overjoyed about the slaying of a couple of sparrows. Evidentially, Hanson, who was somehow totally unaware of the doings at the bank, had picked that inopportune time to shoot a few birds which had been making a nuisance of themselves as of late.

According to news reports, nearly 50 citizens hastily piled into a variety of cars and trucks and began hotly pursuing the bandits' trail. About three miles north of town a carload of officers came upon the robbers attempting to set fire to their rig on the side of the road. On sighting the posse, the highwaymen bolted into the nearby heavy woods. Deputy Sheriff Joe Foreman, and City Marshal Steve Foreman, along with an auto repairman named Herman Greathouse took to the timber afoot, hot on the outlaws' heels, firing rifles and shotguns as they ran. One of the fugitives, struck by a load of birdshot, dropped a feed sack containing about $1,300 in mostly silver, which officers estimated weighed between fifty and sixty pounds, before righting himself and sliding down an embankment into a slough area. The trio of posse men, now out of ammo, grabbed the money sack and retreated to town to resupply.

Within minutes, the rest of the posse arrived in the area. After an hour searching the woods, a group of ten lawmen and volunteers cornered two of the bandits in a small gravel pit pinning them down with a furious stream of gunfire. After firing an estimated sixty rounds in the direction of the trapped fugitives, the pair surrendered, shouting at the posse, "We give up, come on in, we won't shoot." On approaching the desperadoes, lawmen noticed both men were sweating and panting profusely, obviously exhausted by their ordeal. One of the men, who identified himself as Charlie Brackett, was suffering from a gunshot wound to the right shoulder. The second individual who was later identified as Bushyhead (Bush) Wood, cursed the officers as they tried to handcuff him. A vigilante standing nearby responded by smashing him in the face with a pistol butt, breaking his nose. The pair was then transported to the Mayes County Jail in nearby Pryor. When searching the contents of a leather bag found in the duo's possession, officers not only discovered the rest of the loot (the paper money and bonds) intact but a loaf of bread, some coffee beans, and bacon. The bandits had obviously figured to make a day of it.

Towards nightfall, a group of man hunters who had continued the search came across the third bank robber attempting to curl up and hide in a hollow tree, a mile north of where his companions had been captured. The bandit, who had reportedly been struck by several shotgun pellets in the left arm and chest, gave up peaceably. In response to questioning, he admitted his name was Curtis E. Hayes of Barber, Oklahoma.

Deep in the dreary confines of the Mayes County jail Bush Wood, whose broken nose was reportedly bleeding like a "stuck hog," continued to be uncooperative refusing to discuss the robbery, but his comrade and incidentally his cousin, Charlie Brackett, turned out to be a veritable songbird. In a statement made to Justice of the Peace E. A. Church shortly after his arrest, Brackett not only confessed his obvious complicity in the Locust Grove job, but admitted to being in on the Harrison, Arkansas robbery with Henry Starr, Ed Lockhart, and Rufus Rollen as well. He also cursed Starr for "double crossing" him and his fellow robbers, calling the "Bandit King" a "lowdown snitch." He went on to admit he had been hiding out near Barber for the past few months and he and his

Bush Wood. Courtesy-Dian Schwanz.

two crime partners along with three unnamed conspirators had been planning the Locust Grove robbery for over a month. The bandit refused to divulge the names of the mysterious trio he claimed had assisted the robbers in the heist. When questioned, Curtis Hayes, who was "Cotton" Walker's son-in-law, admitted the plan was to burn their car on the roadside and walk to a point where their unnamed crime-partners were to pick them up. He acknowledged the rendezvous was unsuccessful due to the posse being "Right on our ass." Like his companions, Hayes also refused to divulge the names of the unknown conspirators. The two witnesses from the robbery both positively identified Wood and Brackett as the two armed men who had been inside the bank during the robbery.

Over the next few days, Brackett allowed himself to be interviewed by the local press several times. He stated he had a young wife and child currently living in Claremore. When questioned by reporters, the bandit's

Charles Brackett's prison record. Oklahoma Department of Corrections.

attractive spouse claimed she had not seen her husband in months but thought he was hiding out in Mexico and would soon send for her and the child. Asked what her husband was running from, she replied she knew nothing of any robberies, just the fact he had jumped bond on a 1919 attempted murder charge out of Cherokee County. Brackett, sounding like his one time pal Henry Starr, also claimed he had a premonition the Locust Grove job would go badly, but didn't "crawfish" on account of not wanting to appear "chicken" to his companions. The following day, Arkansas officials called for Brackett's extradition to their state to be tried for the Harrison bank robbery. In order to avoid the possibility of doing time in the harsh Arkansas penal system, the bandit promptly pled guilty to the Locust Grove job and was sentenced to ten years at the Oklahoma State pen where he was logged in as inmate #11604.

In the days following the robbery, it was uncovered that Bush Wood had multiple warrants out for his arrest. Authorities suspected him to have been "Kaiser Bill's" companion in both the 1919 robbery of the bank of Gans and the 1920 raid on the Farmers Bank of Gore, Oklahoma. He was also wanted in connection with the recent

Curtis Hayes' prison record. Courtesy Oklahoma Department of Corrections.

robbery of the bank of Cave Springs, Arkansas, as well as several grand larceny charges in Muskogee and Cherokee Counties, Oklahoma. At his court appearance, the bandit, who Muskogee County Sheriff Jim Robbins once characterized as "A real bad Indian," unexpectedly threw himself on the mercy of the court. In response to Wood's request for leniency, the Mayes County attorney remarked, "I do not wish to recommend a sentence which appears to crucify the defendant, nor do I want his last drop of blood, but we can't have him running free robbing our banks and shooting at our officers either!" The judge then sentenced the defendant to ten years hard labor. Curtis Hayes also pled guilty to a charge of armed robbery and for reasons not apparent was hammered with a stiff twenty-year sentence. Hayes entered the Oklahoma pen as inmate #11340 on May 25, 1921.

On news of Hayes' harsh sentence, his father, who had reputably been a long time friend of the late Henry Starr, protested the severity of the Court's ruling. Due to the bandit's impressive record in the World War, his neighbors began gathering names on a petition requesting the Governor reduce the sentence. After several years, the effort proved successful. Oklahoma Governor Jack Walton commuted his sentence on October 10, 1923, to five years.

In the aftermath of the robbery, the owners of the Locust Grove bank were proud as punch of their employee's behavior during the emergency. Evidently, the bank's workers had been drilled numerous times in the past on how to react in a robbery, including how to release themselves from the locked vault. Apparently the bankers had purposely adjusted the interior door where it could be easily opened from inside. When Bank Teller Hatfield was questioned by officers the morning after the robbery, he told them a man similar in appearance to Brackett had approached him the previous week asking for change for a twenty dollar bill. The banker went on to say, an unidentified individual who wore a floppy hat, which partially shielded his face, had accompanied Brackett at the time. Lawmen expressed the opinion that the unknown man was probably Brackett's partner in the Harrison robbery, Ed Lockhart.

With his suspected presence at the Seligman, Harrison, and now Locust Grove robberies, Ed Lockhart became one of the most wanted men in the Midwest. A flurry of all point's bulletins and be on the lookout warnings were wired to law enforcement agencies from Chicago to New Orleans. Three days after the Locust Grove heist, the Chief of Police in Lima, Ohio announced the death of Ed Lockhart. Apparently, the Lima Police had surrounded five men in a vacant downtown warehouse who were suspected of robbing a bank in nearby Huntertown, Indiana. When the desperadoes refused to surrender, the huge posse of lawmen proceeded to assault the building and in the process killed several of the suspects. One of the deceased fit the description of Lockhart. Turns out, the Chief couldn't have been more wrong in his overzealous identification. Apparently, Ed was enjoying a little R and R with his wife at his brother-in-law's home located near the tiny community of St. Joe, Arkansas at the time. Over the next few months, the bandit holed up there and in the Cookson Hills area of Oklahoma keeping a low profile.

On the morning of December 20, 1921, three masked men rode up to the Bank of North Arkansas in the small town of Everton. One man held the horses while the others relieved the institution of nearly $4,000 in cash and gold before making their escape. Due to the bank's proximity to Lockhart's home in nearby St. Joe as well as the physical descriptions given by witnesses, lawmen initially suspected either Ed Lockhart or his little brother Sam as the leader of the desperadoes.

Four hours later and a few hundred miles away, two individuals mounted on horseback rode into the little Illinois River town of Gore, Oklahoma. After tying their horses to a hitching rail behind the Farmers Bank, one man, later known to be Ed Lockhart, stepped into the bank's lobby, which was occupied at the time by the assistant cashier Ira Linders and two witnesses, Mrs. G. B.

Old Gore bank building today, now a floral and gift shop.
Photo by Naomi Morgan.

Foreman and Adam Hendrix. The man, armed with a nickel plated Colt automatic ordered the pair into the vault while his partner, suspected to have been an Arkansas man named Jack Brodie, stood guard at the bank's door watching the street. After shutting (but not locking) the witnesses in the vault, the robbers looted the bank for about $1,600. Within minutes of the robbery, the victims released themselves from their predicament and gave the alarm. Soon afterwards, Sequoyah County Sheriff Goodlow Gay and a posse made up of Deputies Lee Blair, Bullet Fields, and Rufus Smith, arrived on the scene and began following the robbers' trail, which led directly into the rugged Greenleaf Mountains. With the coming of darkness, the lawmen, unable to make out the fugitives tracks, threw in the towel, saying the chase was futile.

According to a statement made by Sheriff Gay, the current set of robbers was not the same ones who had raided the bank twice in the past three years. "They were younger," he claimed. Actually, the financial institution had been hit four times in as many years, first, in 1918 by "Cotton" Walker, "Kaiser Bill," and Mount Cookson, then again in late 1920, in a repeat performance by "Kaiser Bill," aided this time by Bush Wood, and then in September 1921 the unlucky bank was the victim of a nighttime burglary. The fourth robbery was the straw that broke the camel's back. The bank's owners soon threw up their hands and called it quits.

The following day, the owner of a clothing store in Tahlequah, Oklahoma, Mooney Sherman, walked into the office of Chief of Police Perkins stating a suspicious character had just strolled out of his business after buying a new suit of clothes, an expensive gold watch, and a derby. He went on to state, the individual paid cash for the items from a huge wad of dough he had pulled out of his pocket. On receipt of this intelligence, the chief began touring the town looking for the character in question. He soon spotted him sitting on a bench at the Frisco Railroad Depot in all his finery. When questioned, the gentleman informed Perkins his name was Bill Smith, saying he had come to town to do some gambling "with the boys," but had decided to return home to Arkansas on account of his feeling "unlucky." The chief, not buying his explanation, shook the fellow down finding $547 in gold coin and an added $1,300 in greenbacks. Asked where he got the loot, he responded, "Cattle business." The man was promptly arrested and lodged in the town jail for further questioning. Aware of the recent Everton Bank robbery, the chief contacted Arkansas authorities requesting details of the crime. They promptly responded that the exact amount of gold coins taken from the heist corresponded with the sum found on the stranger's person, adding, W. M. Thompson, an employee of the financial institution and a witness to the robbery would be arriving in Tahlequah by morning via railcar in an effort to identify the suspect.

Upon the banker's arrival the following day, he positively identified the prisoner as one of the looters of his

The old Frisco Rail Depot, Tahlequah, Oklahoma. Courtesy Three Rivers Museum, Muskogee, Oklahoma.

place of employment. After some intense grilling, the suspect finally admitted his true name was L.W. Sitton, hailing from Searcy County, Arkansas. Incidentally, he was a relative by marriage to Ed Lockhart. When grilled about the identities of his partners in the robbery, the bad man responded with a big grin and total silence. Sitton was transported back to Boone County, Arkansas where he was promptly convicted of armed robbery and sentenced to ten years in prison.

Back at Harrison, Arkansas, Clarence Bell of Claremore, Oklahoma, and two pals motored into town riding in a Ford Touring car. Bell was determined to retrieve the remains of his bullet smashed, half burned, late model Nash automobile, which had been stolen in mid-February by Henry Starr and the robbers of the Peoples National Bank. Once he located his car, which was in the custody of the Boone County Sheriff's Department, Bell had it towed to a local garage where a mechanic gave the rig a good going over. To the Oklahoman's delight, the car was in surprisingly good shape for what it had been through. Except for the fire-damaged roof and bullet smashed tire and back glass, the Nash was sound, both mechanically and otherwise. Bell had the tire replaced, and with his friends following close behind, drove the vehicle back home to Claremore.

Chapter 5

Hulbert, Park Hill and Pursuit in the Mountains

With the Ozarks caught firmly in the grip of winter, an uneasy quiet settled along the Arkansas-Oklahoma border. In the opening week of January 1922, the Oklahoma Banker's Association posted a $500 reward to be added to the existing $500 offered by the directors of the Peoples Bank of Harrison for Ed Lockhart's capture. The bank at Everton, Arkansas also announced a lesser $250 reward for the arrest of Ed's brother, Sam, and an unnamed companion.

At approximately 12:45 on the afternoon of January 20, 1922, three horsemen rode into the small town of Hulbert, Oklahoma, hitching their horses to a rail located across the street from the First National Bank. Inside the bank, Cashier Clem Hunt was servicing a pair of customers when he looked up noticing three unmasked men enter the bank's lobby armed with revolvers. One of the individuals stated with a loud, clear voice, "Stick 'em up."

While the pair of customers was forced to stand against a wall, Cashier Hunt was ordered to open the door leading to the vault. After harvesting nearly $2,300 from the safe and tills, the bandits forced the witnesses into the vault room. Suddenly, another bank employee named Grover Patterson, who had been out to lunch, entered the building. Catching sight of the bank teller, two of the robbers turned and fired simultaneously at the hapless man

---

with one bullet striking the wall while another hit the door-sill just inches above his head. Unwounded, but near-paralyzed with fear, Patterson was ordered at gunpoint to join the other witnesses in the vault, which was locked behind him.

Several citizens in the street noticed the trio of robbers mount up and slowly ride out of town on a pair of sorrels and a bay. On reaching the edge of the village, the riders spurred their mounts into a gallop. Within minutes of the heist, the witnesses back at the bank freed themselves from the vault with a handy screwdriver and dashed into the street giving the alarm. Constable Jim Burt and an Anti-Horse-Theft officer promptly mounted and followed the bandits' trail for several miles before loosing sight of the outlaws when they plunged into a stretch of thick, deep timber south of town.

A delay was encountered in contacting the county sheriff's office in nearby Tahlequah, due to the telephone wires being cut leading out of town. About two hours after the raid, Cherokee County Deputies Jay Fellows and Jerry Powell arrived in Hulbert. Traveling in a Model "T" Roadster, the lawmen immediately drove to a point near Park Hill hoping to cut off the bandits who they figured were heading toward their lair in the Cooksons. Turns out, the officers were correct in their assumption. Although the pair twice spotted the fugitives, they were never able to get within shooting distance.

Sheriff George Gourd showed up in Hulbert later that afternoon with a large posse. After scouring the district for a night and a day, the cold and hungry posse became discouraged and disbanded. Deputies Fellows and Powell remained in the field for the remainder of the week searching the Pettit and Qualls areas.

Several days after the Hulbert raid, Sheriff Gourd in a statement to the press, claimed the robbery was the work of the "Cookson Bunch." The lawman elaborated, telling the assembled newsmen, the same band of robbers had recently stuck up the Gore bank as well as the banks in Gans, Oklahoma and Everton, Arkansas.

Five days later on the cold snowy morning of January 25, two men dressed in bib overalls, one donning a mask and both sporting automatic pistols entered the Farmers State Bank of Park Hill, located just south

Cherokee County Sheriff George Gourd. Courtesy Cherokee County Sheriff's Department.

of Tahlequah. Cashier T. L. Ballenger, who was the only person in the bank at the time, was forced at gunpoint to open the door of the vault. One of the robbers apologized for the holdup, telling the cashier it was "hardin times." As one of the individuals stood guard in the lobby, the other rifled the vault and cash drawers for approximately $570 in cash and coin. Upon completion of the robbery the pair walked out a side door, one mounted a coal black mare and the other a bald faced sorrel. Witnesses sighted the duo galloping out of town heading towards the nearby Illinois River. Responding to the emergency, a large posse of over thirty vigilantes set out on both horseback and automobile towards the heavily timbered river bottom following the bandit's well-marked trail.

Cherokee County Sheriff George Gourd along with Chief Field Deputy Jay Fellows, and Deputies Jerry Powell, Bill Johnson, and Bob Woodall soon joined the posse. Around dusk, the fugitives were spotted near the river two and a half miles northeast of Park Hill. The group of officers and vigilantes quickly opened up on the bandits with a variety of weapons, wounding the bald face

---

sorrel one of the men was riding. The horse went down roughly throwing its rider into the dirt. Turning their attention to his companion riding the black mare, the group fired another volley, one round striking the horse in the right ear. The mare reacted by falling flat on her chest before rolling on its back spilling her passenger into an oak tree. Both fugitives, now afoot, fled into a heavily thicketed area. The posse, only a couple of hundred yards behind the outlaws, soon captured the men's mounts. Fig-

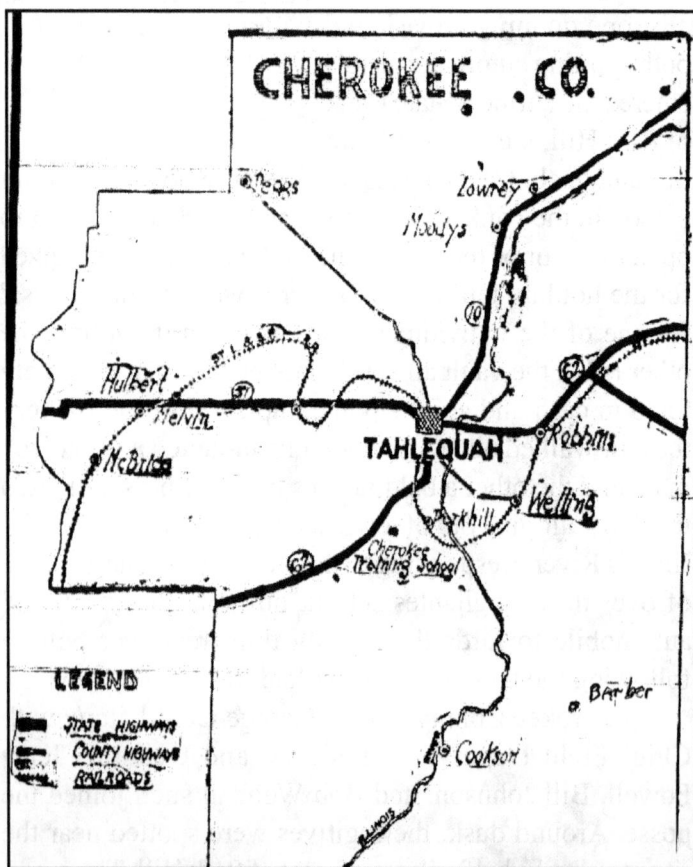

Map Cherokee County, Oklahoma, at the time of the robberies.
Courtesy Tahlequah Leader-Arrow.

uring they had the bandits over the barrel, Gourd ordered the posse to spread out in an effort to surround their quarry. Once the area was encircled, the vigilantes were ordered to stay put and wait for daylight before charging the thicket. Unluckily for the lawmen, sometime during the night the suspects slipped out of the trap, crossing to the east side of the Illinois River.

The following morning when lawmen were able to get a better look at the suspect's injured mounts; officers noticed the sorrel was suffering from a severe neck wound. Sheriff Gourd drew his pistol destroying the injured animal before turning his attention to the slightly wounded black mare. The Sheriff observed the mare's saddle was stamped "W. D. Brewer Muskogee, Saddle Maker." Searching the discarded saddlebags, lawmen could find no clue of the identities of the fugitives. Gourd decided to let the black mare loose hoping it would find its way home in search of a ration of oats. He instructed Deputy Fellows and a small party of officers to shadow the pony wherever it led them. Gourd, who had been in the field enduring the freezing-cold, icy environment for over twenty-four hours, had taken ill and was forced to seek medical attention. Fellows and his mates freed the black horse following its tracks in the snow a half-mile south, then across the river at Turner's Ford near the Frisco rail bridge.

Trailing behind the mare at an average distance of a quarter mile the posse slowly made their way into the snow covered Cookson Hills. Near the community of Barber, they were joined by fellow lawmen, Joe Lee Smith and Roy Eastman. After another sixteen hours and twenty miles in the saddle, enduring a cold driving wind and frozen sleet slapping them in the face like birdshot, the officers observed the horse stumble into the front yard of the Jess Blair residence and drop down on all four knees

Cherokee County Deputy Sheriff Jay Fellows. Courtesy Muskogee Democrat.

in total exhaustion. After surrounding the cabin, Deputy Jerry Powell called for Blair to come outside and talk to them, which he did. Blair admitted ownership of the horse, but denied any involvement with any robbery. Although the authorities at the time were convinced Blair was somehow tied into the robbery, there was scant evidence to prove it.

After placing Blair under arrest, the posse headed back toward the county seat in Tahlequah. Just south of the Standing Rock area, they spotted two men on horseback riding east toward Barber. On questioning the men, they gave their names as George and William Price of nearby Cookson. When asked why the pair was carrying pistols and high-powered Winchester rifles, they responded, "we're deer hunting." Searching their bags, Fellows came across a pair of lineman's pliers and twenty-five shiny-new silver half dollars (100 newly minted half-dollar coins were stolen from the Hulbert bank). When quizzed about their possession of the cutting tool and newly minted coins, George Price became indignant, stating, "None of your damn business." Since the men were riding sorrel horses matching the physical descriptions of those used in the Hulbert robbery, the chief deputy and his posse disarmed the pair placing them under arrest for suspicion of bank robbery. The mounted group, now numbering nine headed west, crossed the icy Illinois River, slowly slogging through the drifting snow toward the county seat of justice.

Posse and prisoners standing in front of Cherokee County courthouse, Deputy Jerry Powell, far left. Courtesy Muskogee Phoenix.

On arrival at the courthouse in Tahlequah, the exhausted posse was disbanded and Blair and the Price boys were tossed into the county jail. The following day Sheriff George Gourd commenting to reporters on the arduous horse-shadowing job his deputies had just completed was quoted as saying, "I guess that horse was a plumb failure as a bloodhound. I had hoped the nag would lead us to the actual robbers not just its owner."

After being vigorously interrogated for several days, the Price brothers were released from custody due to failure of the Hulbert bankers to positively identify them. Blair was charged with obstructing justice and remained lodged in the county "Steel Bar Hotel" awaiting trial. The Park Hill bank announced a $1000 cash reward for the arrest of the varmints who had plundered their institution. The following day, the bank in Hulbert matched the offer.

The big break in the case came on the evening of February 2, when a citizen named Harry Sewell, caretaker at the nearby Sequoyah Club, contacted Undersheriff Jay Fellows informing him of a carload of individuals acting in a peculiar manner at the foot of the nearby Frisco rail bridge. Adding: "They appeared to be searching for something in the brush." Figuring the men were bootleggers, Fellows grabbed Jailor Oscar Woodall and sped to the club where Sewell and L. W. Smith offered to guide the pair to the last spot they had seen the suspicious rig. On approaching the bridge in two cars, the officers sighted the car in question. Parking directly in front of the automobile, Fellows could make out three figures sitting stone still in the car's front seat. When the deputy ordered the individuals to slide out the car with their hands in the air, the driver attempted to start the rig. Fellows reacted by leaping out of his cruiser firing a full clip from his Colt .45 automatic pistol into the automobile, smashing the front windshield and headlights. Within seconds, all three of the car's passengers "got religion," hopping out of the car with their hands pointed skyward in submission.

When questioned, the suspects gave their names as Lewis Curtis of Braggs, Buster Sumpter, and George Salmon. Asked what they were up to, the men declined to answer. The pair of lawmen then handcuffed the trio and stuffed them into the back seat of their patrol car for transport to the county jail in Tahlequah where they could be more closely questioned. Before leaving the scene, Fellows asked Smith and Sewell to search the suspect's car and get back to him if they found anything interesting. Within minutes of the officer's arrival at the jail, a phone message was received from Sewell, requesting the lawmen immediately return to the scene. Fellows, now joined by Sheriff Gourd, rushed back to the location of the abandoned automobile. Upon the officer's arrival, Sewell and

*Lewis Curtis, far left, and companions. Courtesy Muskogee
Democrat*

Smith opened the trunk of the suspect's car and presented
the Sheriff with a burlap bag containing $134.52 in change
along with a loose wrapper stamped "Property of the
Farmers State Bank of Park Hill."

Back at the jail, the three subjects denied any knowledge of the loot. The following morning the authorities
brought in their big gun, Ex-Congressman W. W. Hastings,
who had been appointed the state's council in the affair.
Hastings, who was a man of immense persuasive powers,
commenced to interrogate the men one at a time. He began with Lewis Curtis, who admitted he was twenty-eight-
years of age and married with four children. He further
stated he resided in the community of Braggs where he
operated a barbershop. After several hours of intense questioning, Curtis caved in, launching into an eight-hour soul

searching confession in which he implicated himself, as well as a multitude of citizens for their alleged involvement in the Park Hill heist.

He began his rambling statement by recounting a meeting between him, "Cotton" Walker, and Berry Dotson in a poolroom at the Southern Hotel in Muskogee several months previously. Curtis claimed the pair had fleeced him out of his life savings in a game of stud poker later that same evening. Afterwards, Walker had allegedly inquired if he wanted an opportunity to get his money back. Naturally, the barber quickly replied in the affirmative. According to Curtis, "Cotton" explained he needed a man to help rob a bank. The youthful informant went on to state; he and a twenty-eight-year-old Sequoyah County man named Charley White (alias James Gibson) traveled with Walker, Dotson, and a man named McDougal by train to Everton and Jasper, Arkansas where "Cotton" and Dotson scouted out the local banks. Not seeing what they liked, the group traveled back to Tahlequah by rail before riding to Walker's home near Barber. It was at that point the little storekeeper decided they would hit the Park Hill bank. Incidentally, Curtis stated, while in Arkansas the group took a detour into Searcy County where they met with Ed Lockhart at his father-in-law's residence. Also in attendance was L.W. Sitton and an individual who claimed his name was Jack Jackson.

Asked how the robbery was planned, Curtis explained, "Walker rode into Park Hill to case the bank. He told us he was too well known in the community to participate in the robbery, but it would be like taking candy from a child. Afterwards he loaned Charley a horse and purchased a little black mare for $25 from Jess Blair for me to ride." Walker then cautioned the twosome, "If you birds don't go through with the job, I'll black my face and do it myself. I'm not afraid of a little gunplay!" According to Curtis, Walker informed the pair the bank was currently storing a large number of gold coins, before sending them on their way with a final admonition to make sure he got his fair share of the loot. With that said, young Lewis stopped talking and began to visibly tremble, telling Hastings: "I'm not a bad man, just easily fooled by others."

When the prosecutor prodded him to come clean and tell the whole story, Curtis stood up and walked to a closed window where after staring at the ice covered trees on the courthouse lawn for a few moments, he took a big breath to regain his composure before sitting back in his chair. Then, with a look of grim determination on his face he continued his statement, saying: "After leaving 'Cotton's' residence, me and Charley rode to just south of Park Hill where we camped for the night. At first light, we mounted up and began traveling towards town." He added: "About a mile outside Park Hill we met up with a dirt farmer and struck up a conversation which lasted till we arrived at the Mercantile Store where the farmer went on into the store to do some trading while we tied our horses to the pipe and walked to the bank entering through a side door."

Curtis elaborated, stating his companion pulled a stocking halfway down his face in an effort to hide a prominent scar above his right eye, before entering the bank.

The shaken youth continued his confession saying: "On entering the bank we encountered the cashier who we ordered to fill up our sacks with money. That bank teller refused to move, just gave us a blank stare. He was about the nerviest devil I ever saw!" At this junction in the interrogation Curtis sat silent staring into space for several moments as if pondering his predicament before declaring: "Charley had to jam that pistol pretty rough into that banker's ribs to get any action out of him... Then we stuffed all the money we could into a pair of feed sacks before leaving."

When Hastings inquired how the pair was able to escape, the young bandit replied, "We rode about two and a half miles toward the river, then stopped for lunch and began counting the loot. Looking into the bags, we was mighty disappointed to find mainly pennies and nickels in one of the sacks." He further stated: "We figured them pokes were so heavy due to them being loaded down with the gold coins Walker promised we would find... One sack did have mostly paper money in it"

According to Curtis, while the pair was taking inventory of the "swag," the posse rode up. Reacting to their arrival, they quickly mounted their steeds and began fleeing in the direction of the nearby Illinois River crossing at Turner's Ford. When the sorrel White was riding was shot, flinging the bandit tumbling headfirst into the frozen earth, he promptly abandoned the wounded animal and grabbed the moneybags. Within seconds of his partner's horse being wounded, Curtis was thrown to the ground when a bullet smashed into his mount's right ear. Both fugitives, now a foot, ran a half-mile through the brambles to the river crossing, splashing through the freezing water toward the opposite shore. On reaching the east side of the river the pair hid the heavier bag of booty containing the change under a hollow log and fled south with the sack containing the currency toward Barber and Fred Walker's.

When crowded by Hastings as to the pair's next move, Curtis responded by saying "After tramping all day without food and water, we made our way to Walker's place about sundown. When we saw a burning lantern setting on the porch, (which they took as a warning) we continued walking another hour or two till we come to a home that was occupied by friends of Charley's."

Asked what happened after arriving at the residence, Curtis declared he and his pal collapsed in total exhaustion at the foot of their potbellied stove. On waking the following morning, Curtis claimed he told the man of the house the complete story of the robbery before giving him Walker's cut of the loot, (about $180) and requested he deliver it to the pudgy crook. The pair then continued south on foot till they hit Charley White's residence near Marble City where they split up, both men taking around $130 each with them as their shares.

From Marble City, Curtis claimed he traveled to his mother's house located north of Braggs where he connected with his half-brother George Salmon. A few days later Curtis and Buster Sumpter borrowed Salmon's second hand car, driving to the bridge where they began searching for the hidden loot which amounted to roughly $135 in mostly loose change.

On the morning of February 7, Charley White was captured sitting on the back porch of a relative's home near Marble City. When his elderly father, who lived in rural McIntosh County, Oklahoma, was contacted with news of his son's arrest, he hurriedly traveled to Tahlequah where he convinced the young man to confess his part in the robbery. Although the statement given by White was filled with less detail and gave fewer names, it dovetailed that of his partner. In response to the dual confessions, seventeen warrants were issued for those the law considered culpable in the robbery and its immediate aftermath. Most of those charged, including Curtis's companions, Salmon and Sumpter, quickly bonded out of jail and the county attorney never pursued the charges against them.

A few days after making his dramatic declaration, Curtis added to his confession stating he also had intimate knowledge of the recent bank robberies at Locust Grove, Hulbert, and Gore, Oklahoma as well as Everton,

---

FELONY
COMPLAINT FOR MISDEMEANOR

THE STATE OF OKLAHOMA, } ss.
County of Cherokee.

Before A.E.Robertson, Judge of the Court of Cherokee County, and State of Oklahoma, comes _____ Asbery Burkhead, Co. Attorney _____ and makes complaint on oath and says, that on the or about the 25th day of _____ January, 1922, _____ in said County of Cherokee and State of Oklahoma, _____ Fred Walker, Louis Curtis and James Gibson, alias Charley White, _____

did then and there commit the crime of conjoint robbery in manner and form as follows, to-wit:

That is to say, the said Fred Walker, Louis Curtis and James Gibson alias Charley White, in Cherokee county, State of Oklahoma, then and there being, on or about the 25th day of January, 1922, did, then and there in and upon one T.L.Ballinger, conjointly, wilfully, wrongfully and feloniously, make an assault with revolvers, the same dangerous and deadly weapons, which the said Fred Walker, Louis Curtis and James Gibson, alias Charley White, then and there, held in their hands, and therewith, and by violence and threats, put the said T.L.Ballinger, in fear of unlawful and immediate injury to his person and property, and the property of the Farmers State Bank of Park Hill, a corporation, of which the said T.L. Ballinger, was then and there, its cashier and custodian of its property, thereby and by the force and threats, aforesaid, did, then and there, produce in the mind of said T.L.Ballinger, such fear of unlawful and immediate injury to his person, as was sufficient to, and did, overcome all resistance on the part of the said T.L.Ballinger, and while said T.L.Ballinger was, so as aforesaid, held under such fear by the means aforesaid, the said Fred Walker, Louis Curtis and James Gibson, alias Charley White, did then and there, unlawfully, wilfully and feloniously and conjointly, rob, steal take and carry away, off and from the person and possession and from the immediate presence of the said T.L.Ballinger, the sum of $570.00; good and lawful money of the United States, and of the actual value of $570.00, against the will and without the consent of the said T.L.Ballinger and the said Farmers State Bank of Park Hill, Okla., with the unlawful and felonious intent of them, the said Fred Walker, Louis Curtis, to deprive the true owner thereof, and to convert the same to their own use.

contrary to the form of the Statute in such case made and provided, and against the peace and dignity of the State of Oklahoma.

Wherefore he prays that a warrant may issue commanding the arrest of the said Fred Walker Charley White that they Louis Curtis and James Gibson, alias _____ may be dealt with according to law.

Asbery Burkhead
Co. attorney

Subscribed and sworn to before me this 9th day of February, 1922.

A.E.Robertson

County Judge.

I have examined the facts in this case and recommend that a warrant do issue.

Asbery Burkhead
County Attorney.

Felony complaint against Fred Walker, Lewis Curtis and Charley White for Park Hill robbery. Courtesy Cherokee County Court Clerk.

Arkansas, claiming he had overheard Walker and others recount the robberies in detail. Curtis claimed Walker had planned all four-bank raids. As for the actual players in the robberies, he named Jack Jackson and Ed Lockhart, along with either Jack Brodie (sometimes spelled Brody or Broady) or George Price as the guilty parties in the Hulbert job. He also claimed Mount Cookson had aided the Hulbert robbers in making their escape. Furthermore, Curtis insisted Lockhart, with the aide of Jack Brodie had pulled off the most recent Gore bank heist and Ed's brother Sam, along with L.W. Sitton, (who was already in custody) and possibly Jack Jackson had hijacked the Everton bank. The talkative informer further declared Walker had revealed to him the fact that he, Berry Dotson, and Ed Lockhart were the long sought unnamed coconspirators in the 1921 Locust Grove bank robbery. At the time of the bank raid, two of the three bandits admitted when captured they were in the process of making their way on foot to another vehicle which had been stationed a mile or so from where they had abandoned and set fire to their own getaway car. Since neither robber would confess to the identity of the occupants of the second car, Mayes County investigators were stymied in their efforts to prosecute their mysterious crime-partners. Upon being confronted with Curtis's latest disclosure, Charley White confirmed most of the details contained in his long-winded partner's story.

In response to these latter revelations, felony arrest warrants were issued from Mayes, Cherokee, and Sequoyah Counties for Fred Walker, Berry and Bee Dotson, Ed Lockhart, Jack Brodie, George E. (Jack) Jackson, George Price, and Mount Cookson. Upon hearing of Curtis's latest confession, area newspapers dubbed the members of the alleged bank robbing conspiracy the "Cookson Gang," due to several of the named individuals residing near the small Cherokee County village of Cookson.

By the time lawmen got around to raiding Walker's home the slippery con man was nowhere to be seen. Arkansas authorities were contacted asking for their assistance in locating Ed Lockhart and others. Officers also swooped down on Mount Cookson's residence, but like Fred Walker, he had flown the coop. Due to his suspected involvement in the Hulbert robbery, Oklahoma's Governor immediately revoked his appeal bond, which he had been under since his 1918 conviction for the Gore bank heist.

In the early morning hours of February 9, Deputy Sheriff Joe Lee Smith received a call from a garage in Hulbert informing him of the presence of Walker, Berry Dotson and his son, Bee. Apparently, the trio had pulled into the shop to have a tire repaired. Smith responded by

Arrest warrant for Mont (Mount) Cookson. Courtesy Cherokee County Court Clerk.

deputizing a small posse of citizens and rushed to the garage. The trio was taken without incident and transported to Tahlequah for questioning. On receipt of the fugitives, Sheriff Gourd announced he had so many charges pending against "Cotton Top" he didn't know where to start.

Four hours later and twenty-five miles north, two masked men wearing long coats entered the Adair (Oklahoma) State Bank. The assistant teller, Faye Godsey, was the only person in the building at the time. According to her statement, she looked up from her bookkeeping noticing the gents; one dressed in bib overalls under his coat and the other, a young man wearing a "cowboy" hat. She went on to say, the oldest of the pair strolled up to her thrusting a pistol in her face, ordering her to "Get 'em up or be damned." Scared out of her wits, the young lady did as she was told while observing the younger individual walk behind the counter and begin looting the cash tills for roughly $1500 in cash and gold coin. Noticing she

Arrest warrant for Jack Brody. Courtesy Cherokee County Court Clerk.

Adair State Bank. Courtesy Mayes County Historical Society.

was about to collapse from fear, the young fellow told her "Calm down, we'll not hurt you, we hate to do this but we must." With that said, he shut her in the vault but left the door cracked. The pair then fled to the rear of the bank and according to witnesses standing in the street, hopped into a Marmon motor car with Missouri tags, being driven by a third man who also wore a mask.

After a short delay, due to the phone lines around town being cut, a message was delivered to the Sheriff's office in Pryor. A string of roadblocks was set up throughout the area, but in the end they proved fruitless. When officers questioned Miss Godsey, she commented the younger bandit had been perfectly "charming" toward her.

The day following the Adair robbery, Charley White, who was presently sitting it out in the Cherokee County Jail awaiting sentencing for his part in the Park Hill robbery, asked to have a word with Prosecutor Hastings. Hoping the young man was having a sudden desire to further clear his conscience, Hastings rushed to the jailhouse, pen in hand. White, hoping to further reduce his sentence, told the prosecutor of a visit he had paid Fred

Walker a few days before his capture. According to White, shortly after his arrival at "Cotton's" home, Berry Dotson, accompanied by a man named Tom Dodd (a pseudonym) drove up. Later that evening he overheard the trio planning the recent Adair bank robbery.

The following day, a posse led by the flamboyant Delaware County Sheriff Ben F. Smith, acting on information provided by Charley White and others, raided a residence near Summers, Arkansas, a small hamlet located on the eastern edge of the Cherokee Hills. Captured in the raid was thirty-nine-year old Tom Dodd of nearby Westville, Oklahoma, along with B. A. Robbie of Joplin, Missouri. The day after the arrests, Charley White did a 180-degree turnaround and suddenly recanted his testimony. Although the county prosecutor was certain they had the guilty parties in custody, he was forced to drop the charges and release the pair of suspects due to lack of evidence.

On February 15, Jay Fellows traveled to Searcy County, Arkansas, arresting George (alias Jack or Ernest) Jackson, a suspect in the Hulbert robbery, at his home in the tiny community of Pindale. Incidentally, Pindale was also the hometown of Troy Love, who would one day evolve into one of the most deadly and elusive outlaws of the 1930s depression era Midwest crime wave. Jackson, who was apparently some sort of relative of Ed Lockhart's, was described by lawmen as six-foot, 180 pounds, blond hair, blue eyes, and possessing several gold-capped teeth. The prisoner was also noted as a professional gambler (like Walker he was partial to stud poker) and a convicted horse thief. The prisoner was transported to Fort Smith where he and the deputy sat several days awaiting extradition papers.

On the 17th, authorities in Huntsville, Arkansas, reported the apprehension of Ed Lockhart and Jack Brodie.

The pair was spotted riding through the town square by a Madison County deputy. Both men were mounted on horses, which had been reported stolen from Marble City, Oklahoma in the immediate aftermath of the recent wave of robberies. In response to the pair's capture, lawmen in Cherokee and Sequoyah Counties, Oklahoma, as well as Boone County, Arkansas requested the company of both men. After the smoke cleared, Arkansas took care of its own, sending Lockhart to Harrison to face the music over the February 1921, Peoples Bank job. Brodie joined Jack Jackson in Fort Smith to await extradition to Oklahoma in connection to the recent Gore and Hulbert robberies.

Twenty-four hours after Lockhart's capture, Cherokee County Sheriff George Gourd arrested Mount Cookson at a residence in Stilwell, Oklahoma. Due to his appeal bond being recently revoked, he was immediately sent to the Oklahoma State Pen to start his five-year sentence (inmate # 12060) for his part in the 1918 Gore bank raid.

Oklahoma Prison record for Mount Cookson. Courtesy Oklahoma Department of Corrections.

Chapter 6

Trial and Punishment, The Muldrow Raid and Armed Men Mounted on Blooded Horses

In late February 1922, the state of Oklahoma initiated the first of several trials, which took place in Tahlequah, concerning the defendants allegedly involved in the recent spat of bank robberies. The opening case on the docket was that of Lewis Curtis, the twenty-five-year-old Braggs barber. Curtis, who emptied his soul to prosecutors and in doing so implicated what seemed like half the county's citizens, stood before the bar of justice on the afternoon of February 25, 1922. When asked how he pled, he meekly responded guilty. The District Judge, J. H. Jarman of Sallisaw, proceeded to give the young miscreant a short lecture telling him, "I feel I am visiting this sentence on your poor penniless wife and her babies (one being born the day after the robbery) but I have no choice." When the jurist concluded his statement, he peered at Curtis's wife, telling her, "The innocent suffer the most in this world." Asked if he wished to address the court before sentencing, the young defendant rose and began to speak haltingly, pausing every few seconds to regain his composure, saying "I wish I could take it all back, what a damn fool I have been. I blame gambling for my downfall. Walker had convinced me I would make my fortune if I followed his plan. All I wanted was enough money to start a dry goods store in Braggs. I have learned my lesson. A few weeks ago a little girl was born in our house, I've never seen her. Perhaps I have drinking and gambling to thank for that." With that said, Judge Jarman sentenced him to five years hard labor. Curtis was received at the Oklahoma State Penitentiary on March 1, 1922 as inmate #12067.

When the defendant's spouse was interviewed shortly after the verdict, she told reporters, "Lewis has left us in dire straights. If it were not for the generosity of the town grocer, we would starve." She continued her statement saying; "We broke up two years ago when we were living in Arkansas because of his bad habits but got back together and moved to Braggs after he swore he had turned a new leaf. He was sober and industrious until a few months ago when he began to disappear for days on end, leaving me and the children without money, food, or firewood."

Next, to receive his comeuppance was Charley White, who the newspapers claimed to have been a horse-trainer prior to his fall from grace. With his white haired father at his side, he also pled guilty and was in turn give an eight-year prison term. Bank Teller T. L. Ballenger, sitting in the front row of the dusty courtroom, defiantly

		NO. 12067			OSP	28
NAME	Louis Curtis		COLOR	W	AGE	
SENTENCE BEGINS	3-1-22		TERM	5-yrs.		
CRIME	Conjoint Robbery		COUNTY	Cherokee		

witness - Returned

maded. 1932

Paroled Dec. 16, 1922.
Full Pardon 7-23-23

Prison record of Lewis Curtis. Courtesy Oklahoma Department of Corrections.

STATE OF OKLAHOMA)
Cherokee County)

IN DISTRICT COURT

BE IT REMEMBERED, That on the ___20th___ day of _____Feb._____, A. D. 1 _22_, the same

being one of the days of the _____February_____ 19 _22_ Term of the District Court of Cherokee

County, State of Oklahoma, there being present Honorable __J. H. Jarman__, Judge,

___Geo. R. Goard___ Sheriff and ___Geo. Ballew___ Clerk,

and public proclamation of the opening of said Court having been made, the following among other proceedings were had:

THE STATE OF OKLAHOMA
vs.

___Louis Curtis et al___ No. ___1186___

_____
Defendant___

The prisoner, the above named ___Louis Curtis___

defendant, being personally present in open Court, and having been legally __presented by information__

_____for the crime of

__Conjoint Robbery__

and arraigned, and said defendant having entered herein his plea of guilty, as charged in said __Information__

_____, and being asked by the Court if he had any legal cause to show why judgment and sentence should

not be pronounced against him, and he giving no good reason in bar thereof:

IT IS THEREFORE CONSIDERED, ORDERED, ADJUDGED AND DECREED by the Court that the said_____

__Louis Curtis__ be confined in the State Penitentiary at McAlester, in the State of Oklahoma,

for the term of _____Five_____ years, for said crime by him committed, said term of sentence to begin

and from the ___1st___ day of _____March_____ A. D. 19 _22_ and that said defendant

ay the costs of this prosecution, taxed at $_____, for which execution is awarded.

IT IS FURTHER ORDERED, ADJUDGED AND DECREED by the Court that the Sheriff of Cherokee County, State

Oklahoma, transport said ___Louis Curtis___ to the said Penitentiary at McAlester, in the

tate of Oklahoma, and that the Warden of said Penitentiary do confine and imprison the said ___Louis Curtis__

_____ in accordance with this judgment, and that the Clerk of this Court do immediately certify, under

e seal of the Court and deliver to the Sheriff aforesaid, two copies of this judgment, one of said copies to accompany the
dy of said defendant to the said Penitentiary and to be left therewith at said Penitentiary, said copy to be warrant and
thority for the imprisonment of said defendant in said Penitentiary, and the other copy to be the warrant and authority
said Sheriff for the transportation and imprisonment of the said defendant as hereinbefore provided. Said last named
py to be returned to the Clerk of said Court with the proceedings of said Sheriff thereunder endorsed thereon. And thereon the Court notified the defendant of his right of appeal.

Done in open Court on this _____1st_____ day of __March__ 19 _22_

_____ Judge.

*Court judgment decree for Lewis Curtis. Courtesy Cherokee
County Court Clerk.*

STATE OF OKLAHOMA,
CHEROKEE COUNTY.   }   IN DISTRICT COURT.

BE IT REMEMBERED, That on the......1st..........day of...............March...........
A. D., 19..22., the same being one of the days of the.....February.....................19 22.
Term of the District Court of Cherokee County, State of Oklahoma, there being present Honorable
...J. H. Jarman............................Judge, ...Geo. R. Gourd............Sheriff
and......Geo. Ballew........................Clerk, and public proclamation of the opening of said
Court having been made, the following among other proceedings were had:

THE STATE OF OKLAHOMA
            vs.   }
.........Charlie White..............................   No..1186...........
....
                    Defendant....../

The prisoner, the above named....Charlie White..............................
defendant, being personally present in open Court, and having been legally..............
...presented by information...for the crime of
...Conjoint robbery..
and arraigned, and said defendant having entered herein his plea of guilty, as charged in said
....Information.............................., and being asked by the Court if he had any
legal cause to show why judgment and sentence should not be pronounced against him, and he
giving no good reason in bar thereof:

IT IS THEREFORE CONSIDERED, ORDERED, ADJUDGED AND DECREED by the Court

that the said.........Charlie White.............................be confined in the State Penitentiary

at.........McAlester...................., in the State of...Oklahoma.....................

for the term of...........Eight.............years, for said crime by him committed, said term of

sentence to begin at and from the.........1st.....day of............March.............A. D., 19..22.

and that said defendant pay the costs of this prosecution, taxed at $...................., for which
execution is awarded.

IT IS FURTHER ORDERED, ADJUDGED AND DECREED by the Court that the Sheriff of
Cherokee County, State of Oklahoma, transport said.....Charlie White....to the said penitentiary
at....McAlester........in the State of......Oklahoma.....and that the warden of said penitentiary
do confine and imprison the said....Charlie White......in accordance with this judgment, and that
the Clerk of this Court do immediately certify, under the seal of the Court and deliver to the Sheriff
aforesaid, two copies of this judgment, one of said copies to accompany the body of said defendant
to the said penitentiary and to be left therewith at said penitentiary, said copy to be warrant and
authority for the imprisonment of said defendant in said penitentiary, and the other copy to be the
warrant and authority of said Sheriff for the transportation and imprisonment of the said defendant as hereinbefore provided. Said last named copy to be returned to the Clerk of said Court with
the proceedings of said Sheriff thereunder endorsed thereon. And thereupon the Court notified the
defendant of his right of appeal.

Done in open Court on this......1st......day of......March.............19..22.

......J. H. Jarman.....................................Judge

*Judgment decree for Charley White. Courtesy Cherokee County
Court Clerk.*

glared at the bandit as he was led from the room. The following day, the Park Hill bank paid out a $1000 reward to be split between Deputies Fellows and Woodall along with the two Sequoyah Club employees.

On February 27, Fred "Cotton" Walker came to trial. His lawyer immediately asked for a change of venue, claiming his client could never receive a fair trial in Eastern Oklahoma due to statements made by the prosecuting attorney suggesting his client was the mastermind behind the Gans, Hulbert, Park Hill, Gore, Adair, and Locust Grove, Oklahoma robberies. The Prosecutor had also publicly implied Walker had a hand in planning the raids on the bank in Seligman, Missouri, as well as those in Everton and Harrison, Arkansas. Furthermore, Walker's attorney noted recent news stories printed in several major area papers that pointedly stated the brainy storekeeper was the head of a huge gang of highwaymen which had

Subpoenas for Walker's trial. Courtesy Cherokee County Court Clerk.

spread it's tentacles throughout a four state region. The Judge denied the motion. The lawyer then demanded a thirty-day delay in the proceedings. Jarman also promptly rejected this tactical move.

What in fact "Cotton Top" had to do with this long laundry list of crimes was and still is to some extent a mystery. Although it is likely he had some culpability in planning the Oklahoma robberies, it may be a stretch to say the little man played more than a peripheral role if any in the others. It's true that Walker was deeply involved with both Charlie Brackett and Ed Lockhart, who were present at the Harrison and Seligman jobs, but to imply he masterminded these events for Henry Starr and company borders on ludicrous. The idea of an old pro like Starr, who had probably pulled off more bank robberies than any man in American history, taking orders from "Cotton" Walker is farfetched to say the least. What part he played in the Everton, Arkansas bank raid is anyone's guess.

The case the prosecuting attorney presented against Walker consisted of Lewis's and Charley White's confessions along with a great deal of circumstantial evidence. The state had originally hoped Jess Blair would turn state's

Prison record for Fred Walker. Courtesy of Oklahoma Department of Corrections.

Judgment and Sentence on Conviction.

STATE OF OKLAHOMA,
Cherokee County }

IN DISTRICT COURT

BE IT REMEMBERED, That on the ____28_____ day of ____February_____ A. D. 19_22___, the

same being one of the days of the ____February_____ 19_22__ term of the District Court of

Cherokee County, State of Oklahoma, there being present the

Honorable _____J._H._Jarman_____ Judge,

_____Geo._R._Gourd_____ Sheriff

and _____Geo._Ballew_____ Clerk.

And Public proclamation of the opening of said Court having been made, the following among other proceedings
were had:

THE STATE OF OKLAHOMA,
vs.
_____Fred_Walker_et_al_____ } No__1186_____

_____
Defendant____

The prisoner above named (a)_____Fred_Walker_____ defendant,

being personally present in open Court and having been legally __presented_by_information_____

_____

and arraigned and having plead not guilty to the crime of__ ____Conjoint_robbery_____

charged in said _____Information_____ and having been then and there in said Court, duly

and legally tried and convicted of said crime, and upon being asked by the Court whether he had any legal cause to show
why judgment and sentence should not be pronounced against him, and giving no good reason in bar thereof, and none appear-
ing to the Court.

IT IS THEREFORE ORDERED, ADJUDGED AND DECREED by the Court that the said _____Fred_Walker__

_____ be confined in the State

Penitentiary at McAlester, in the State of Oklahoma, for the term of _____Twelve_____ years for said crime

by him committed. Said term of imprisonment to begin at and from the _____1st___ day of ___March_____

_____, A. D. 19_22__, and that said defendant pay the costs of this prosecution for which execution is awarded.

IT IS FURTHER ORDERED, ADJUDGED AND DECREED by the Court that the Sheriff of Cherokee County, State

of Oklahoma, transport said _____Fred_Walker_____ to the said penitentiary at McAlester,

in the State of Oklahoma, and that the warden of said penitentiary do confine and imprison said defendant in accordance
with this judgment, and that the Clerk of this Court do immediately certify, under the seal of the Court, and deliver to
the Sheriff aforesaid, two copies of this judgment, one of said copies to accompany the body of said defendant to the said
penitentiary and to be left therewith, to be warrant and authority for the imprisonment of said defendant in said penitentiary, and the other copy to be the warrant and authority for the transportation and imprisonment of the
said defendant, as hereinbefore provided. Said last named copy to be returned to the Clerk of said Court with the proceedings of said Sheriff thereunder endorsed thereon.

Done in open Court this _____1st_____day of__ ___March_____, 19_22__.

_____ Judge.

NOTE__(a)_Presented by Information or Indicted by a Grand Jury of said County.

_____ Court Clerk of Cherokee County, State of Oklahoma, do
hereby certify the above and foregoing to be a full, true, correct and complete copy of the judgment and sentence in the

case of the State of Oklahoma vs. _____ as the same appears of record in
my office.

IN WITNESS WHEREOF, I have hereunto set my hand and affixed the seal of said Court, this ____1st___

day of_____March_22_____ 19___

_____ Court Clerk.

Judgment decree for Fred Walker. Courtesy Cherokee County Court Clerk.

evidence and testify against the self-styled "flim flam man." They were greatly disappointed when he flatly refused. Regardless, after deliberating slightly over two hours, the jury came back with a verdict of guilty of conspiracy in the Park Hill robbery. Judge Jarman promptly sentenced "Cotton" to twelve years at the Oklahoma State Pen. Walker, who appeared nervous and jumpy throughout his short trial, reacted to the verdict by scowling at the Judge. The defendant's wife, who was a respected teacher employed at the Cave Springs School on Elk Creek, attended every day of the trial with their daughter, the wife of Curtis Hayes (the convicted Locust Grove robber), by her side. Upon hearing the verdict, both mother and daughter burst into tears. From all indications, Mrs. Walker represented another of those innocent victims the Judge had earlier spoken of.

After sentencing, "Cotton" was allowed to speak to the assembled members of the press. He began by protesting the verdict as grossly unfair before launching into a lengthy tirade, condemning "snitches," stating, "If I go to the penitentiary, I'll go straight, I'll not go howling on my friends who trusted me." At the conclusion of Walker's trial, all charges were dropped against Jess Blair, whose only crime seems to have been unwittingly selling a horse to a neighbor.

With the conviction of the Park Hill bandits, Special Prosecutor W.W. Hastings made a statement to the press saying; "We've really cleaned house this time, Cherokee County will no longer be the headquarters for any bank robbing gangs." As history shows us, his crystal ball must have had a crack in it when he made that misguided prediction.

Ironically, within a month of the termination of the Walker trial, the Park Hill bank failed due to internal mismanagement. Evidently, the bank's president had long been engaged in some rather unorthodox bookkeeping practices. He was later convicted of fraud and sentenced to five years in the Oklahoma State Penitentiary.

On March 6, Hulbert Bank Cashier Clem Hunt, who was a witness to the Hulbert bank robbery, accompanied Special prosecutor Hastings to Boone County, Arkansas in order to view Ed Lockhart at the county jail. On taking a quick glance at the desperado, he positively identified him as one of the robbers of his place of employment.

Meanwhile, back in Tahlequah, Berry Dotson and his son Bee, who had both been captured on February 9th in the company of Fred Walker and since held for questioning, were released from custody. The pair, along with Berry's youngest son, Charley, fled the area taking up residence at a farm located four miles west of Ramona, Oklahoma.

Around this time, Cherokee County Sheriff George Gourd ordered his deputies to bring in George and "Tump" Price for questioning. The Sheriff, along with the county attorney was apparently convinced the pair was involved in the recent series of bank robberies. When a large posse commanded by Deputy Fellows raided George's home near Cookson, neither he nor his younger brother were unearthed, apparently the pair had taken to "tall timber." Lawmen suspected the brothers were "scouting" in the hills north of Marble City, Oklahoma in the unsavory company of "Kaiser Bill" Goodman.

At roughly 11 p.m. on the evening of March 13, Ed Lockhart, who had been cooling his heels in the Boone County Jail in Harrison, Arkansas where he was being held for suspicion of robbing the Peoples State Bank in February 1921, stuck up the night jailor with a pistol a relative had smuggled to him. Taking his keeper hostage, he fled three miles on foot in a thick fog before releasing the man and disappearing into the heavily timbered hills.

Although a half dozen hastily formed posses spent the next three days scouring the mountains in search of the slippery bad man, they hit a dry hole. When lawmen searched his cell after his escape, they discovered a note that read "I'm sorry to have to leave, but I'm a day late. You've got my bond so high my friends will never make it." After pulling his "Houdini" act, newspapers in three states, enamored with his daring deeds, proclaimed him the successor to Henry Starr, thus crowning him the new "Bandit King of the Southwest."

The following day, the wheels of justice began to slowly turn against the defendants in the Hulbert robbery case. Officially charged with the bank heist were Mount Cookson, Jack Jackson, Jack Brodie and Ed Lockhart. Strangely, although Lewis Curtis had named him as a possible suspect in the Hulbert raid, George Price was never officially charged in the case, although he continued to be wanted for questioning in the affair. At a hearing held on the afternoon of March 14 before County Judge A. E. Robertson, Charley White and his partner Lewis Curtis along with the witnesses to the robbery gave their respective testimonies. Defendants Jackson and Brodie appeared in person, both pleading not guilty. Cookson missed the event due to his current incarceration in the state pen, as did Ed Lockhart who was presently scouting in parts unknown. At the conclusion of the hearing, Judge Robertson bound the defendants over to the next session of the District Court, setting Jackson and Brodie's bonds at $5000. Jack Jackson, made bond and disappeared. Brodie, who was unable to come up the needed cash for his bail, was transferred to Sequoyah County to answer a charge of   participating in the December, 1921 Gore, Oklahoma bank raid. The week after his arrival, Brodie pled guilty to armed robbery before Judge J. H. Jarman in a Sallisaw courtroom. The bandit was sentenced to ten years in the Oklahoma state pen. As for Mount Cookson, his parole revocation remained in effect. Future developments in the case will show he was probably the recipient

Felony complaint against Lockhart, Brodie, Jackson and Cookson in regards to the Hulbert bank robbery. Courtesy Cherokee County Court Clerk.

of a "bum rap" in regards to his alleged involvement in the Hulbert bank robbery.

With the countryside in an uproar over Lockhart's latest adventures, the Price boys decided the timing was right for another foray into the settlements. At approximately five minutes before noon on the morning of June 2, 1922, three men rode into the town of Muldrow, Oklahoma mounted on a sorrel and a pair of buckskins. Two of the individuals entered the First National Bank, while a third stayed with the horses. Inside the bank, a teller along with a customer, were ordered to "Stand and deliver" by a man wearing a large cowboy hat and armed with a sawed-off double-barreled shotgun. Another individual rushed behind the cages gathering up $2000 in cash and $15,000 in negotiable (easily cashed) Liberty Bonds. Within minutes, the bandits finished their business before fleeing on horseback in a northerly direction.

The two witnesses to the robbery waited a short spell before running into the street giving the alarm. In less than a half hour, most of the male residents of the town including ex-Sequoyah County Sheriff John E. Johnson were armed, mounted, and in hot pursuit. Later that afternoon, the huge posse spotted the trio of fugitives just south

First National Bank of Muldrow, Oklahoma. Courtesy Muldrow City Clerk's office.

of the community of Liberty in a large open field. The vigilantes began hosing down the fleeing bandits with shotgun, pistol, and rifle fire. One of the robber's horses hit the ground rolling, flinging its passenger to the ground. The rider, who turned out to be Reece Price, gained his footing, pulled a long barreled pistol and began exchanging fire with the posse. He was promptly struck in the right arm by a rifle ball and took a full load of birdshot to the ribs. The wounded outlaw fell to the ground for a second time where he laid for a few seconds before suddenly making a mad dash towards his exhausted horse. Just as he pulled himself into the saddle a volley of rifle fire engulfed his position, one round striking his mount in the head and another smacking the fugitive in the buttocks. Horse and rider again crashed to the earth rolling down an embankment coming to rest against a large cedar tree. The posse quickly surrounded the gravely wounded bandit. When ordered to raise his bleeding and broken arms in surrender, he stated, "I can't, you've shot me to pieces."

Meanwhile, the second and third fugitives spurred their horses towards a wooded ravine. With only a four rail wood fence standing between them and the wood line, the pair attempted to jump the barrier with their horses at a full sprint. One man positively identified as Charlie Price leaped over the fence to safety, while the other fugitive crashed into the top two rails, his steed collapsing to the

Ex-Sheriff John E. Johnson. Courtesy Sequoyah County Sheriff's Department.

ground rolling over him. He was immediately put into custody along with his wounded partner. In the meantime, Charlie Price, making it to cover, turned and unloosed a withering barrage of rifle fire on the posse's position wounding three officers. The posse, caught in the open, scattered seeking cover. Price, who must have been well provisioned with ammunition, kept his tormenters pinned down for over a half-hour before fleeing the area. Although the officers were certain young Price was wounded and running low on bullets, they decided not to pursue the bandit into the heavy timber. Instead, they loaded the elder Price brother and his companion, as well as several slightly injured officers into the back of a buckboard heading back to Muldrow with their catch. Upon searching the two wounded thieves, officers discovered the missing $2000 in cash stolen from the bank but were unable to locate the $15,000 in Liberty Bonds.

The following day, the prisoners were transported to Sallisaw for safekeeping and further medical attention. The third bandit, whose horse had rolled over on him af-

Appearance sheet, Reece and Charles Price and Monroe Cook, Charlie no-showed the affair. Courtesy Sequoyah County Clerk's office.

ter attempting to jump the rail fence, was identified as Monroe Cook of Prices Chapel, the son of a prosperous area farmer.

The authorities, believing Charlie would seek refuge with family members near Prices Chapel, dispatched a group of officers, along with two Pinkerton detectives to that community in an effort to cut the outlaw's trail. Unfortunately, for the lawmen, the slippery outlaw who had taken a rifle slug to the elbow stayed clear of his homeplace, instead riding north to the community of Bunch where a Negro horse doctor he had known since childhood provided him medical attention.

Officers, suspecting Charlie was now running with his older brother, raided the home of George Price near Cookson the following day. They drew a blank for their efforts. Although the Muldrow Bank posted a $500 reward for his capture and a battalion of detectives was scouring every nook and cranny in the hills, no sign was seen of the fugitive for nearly a month.

On Monday, the afternoon of July 3rd a ten-man posse led by Sheriff Goodlow Gay of Sallisaw arrived in four Model "T" automobiles at the residence of Jim Harden, located on Dry Creek, five miles east of Marble City. Acting on an informant's tip, the group, which included Sallisaw Chief of Police Mose Newman and Federal Marshal Joe Morgan, surrounded Harden's house, calling out for Price to surrender. Suddenly, the lawmen spotted the fugitive leaping out the window of a nearby church, which was located about fifty yards from the home, and mount a horse that was tethered nearby. Within seconds, both horse and rider had disappeared into the thick brush. Marshal Morgan, running to the spot where he saw the fugitive enter the woods, fired several rounds at the fleeing desperado when he caught a momentary glimpse of the outlaw spurring his horse down an adjacent gully. Price turned and emptied an automatic pistol in Morgan's direction, shooting the Marshal's hat off his head and nicking his ear.

Officers, cursing their luck, decided not to pursue the elusive bandit on foot claiming it was too near dusk, instead they figured to take up the trail at first light. Entering the nearby church, lawmen discovered George Price sitting on a bench. Although, Price was held on charges of harboring as well as his alleged participation in the Hulbert bank robbery, due to a legal technicality he was allowed to make bond within hours of his arrest.

In the month of August, Charlie Price was spotted at both a barn dance in the tiny Cookson Hills settlement of Bunch and sparking a gal who lived on nearby Greasy Creek. By the time lawmen arrived at both locations the elusive bandit was long gone. An informant told officers the flamboyant outlaw was mounted on a blooded horse, which had won numerous races in the area over the past year. He also noted the fugitive was carrying three pistols on his person and a 44-40 caliber Winchester rifle tied to his saddle.

Back in Sallisaw, both Reece Price and Monroe Cook pled guilty to the Muldrow Bank robbery and were sentenced to twenty years apiece at the state rock pile.

NAME Sam Lockhart NO. 11874 OSP
SENTENCE BEGINS - 1-9-22   COLOR W   AGE 28
CRIME Assault to Kill   TERM 1 year   COUNTY Oklahoma.

Discharged 8-19-22

Oklahoma prison record of Sam Lockhart. Courtesy of Oklahoma Department of Corrections.

The following day, the Oklahoma Banker's Association increased the reward for the capture of Charlie Price to $1000. For the next few weeks, the bandit hid out in the hills planning his next move. Around this time George Price, who was presently free on bail, decided to join Charlie on his next robbery. Three of George's acquaintances, twenty-five-year-old Syra "Si" Wilson along with thirty-seven-year-old John Cowan, both of Cookson, (both men lived within a mile of George Price's home) and twenty-one-year-old Mark Hendricks, a farmer residing in nearby Park Hill, Oklahoma, were also seduced into the scheme. On this particular occasion, the brothers decided to modernize their equipment replacing their trusty horses with an automobile as a means of attack and evasion.

While the Price boys planned their next move, Ed Lockhart and his brother Sam, who had been paroled on August 19th from the Oklahoma State pen where he had served eight months of a one year term on an assault to kill charge, traveled to the small Ozark mountain village of Hollister, Missouri, intent on robbing the local bank. After scouting out the financial institution, the pair motored across the White River Bridge to the nearby community of Branson. Parking on Main Street, Ed strolled into a small store looking to purchase some cheese and crackers for lunch, while Sam sat in the automobile with the motor running. Unfortunately, a passing town constable alertly noticed the car the bandit was sitting in matched the description of a vehicle that had been reported as stolen from a Ford dealership in Sallisaw, Oklahoma the previous night. While the lawman was busy getting the drop on his brother, Ed took advantage of the ensuing confusion, slipping out of the store unseen taking off to parts unknown. Sam, enjoying only a few days of freedom since his parole from McAlester, spent the evening staring at the cold steel bars of the Taney County Jail in nearby Forsyth. After spending a few weeks in the county lockup, Sam was mysteriously released from custody.

Chapter 7

Massacre in Eureka Springs

On the early fall afternoon of September 25, 1922, a party of men which included Charlie and George Price, as well as John Cowen and Marcus Hendricks crammed into a large open Model "T" Touring Sedan, heading northeast from Cookson, Oklahoma, into the hills of Arkansas. Around dusk, the men stopped and camped on Leatherwood Creek located just west of the picturesque community of Eureka Springs. According to several sources, Si Wilson joined the group the following morning, arriving in a small Ford Coupe. Who accompanied Wilson on the trip or if he came alone remains a mystery.

That afternoon, Charlie Price and Wilson motored into the town's center. After traveling up a curvy, hillside road named Spring Street; they parked their car in front of the First National Bank. Charlie strolled into the financial institution walking directly to the cashier's counter where he changed a ten dollar note for two fives, his eyes and ears taking in every piece of intelligence he could absorb. Rumor has it that after casing the bank the pair stopped at the nearby Southern Hotel for a relaxing game of stud poker. Toward evening the two drove their planned getaway route before motoring back to the campground informing the others the plan was set and everyone should get a good nights rest.

The following day, five of the desperadoes piled into the Model "T" and drove to the bank, parking across the street with the car headed downhill. At 11:05 am, the Price boys along with Cowen entered the financial institution with guns drawn while Wilson took up a position just inside the front door. Young Hendricks was instructed to stay at the wheel of the vehicle and keep the motor running. Crowds of people were milling in the street while Cashier E. T. Smith, Teller Fred Sawyer, and three clerks, Maude Shuman, Jewel Davidson, and Loma Sawyer were busily going about their jobs in the

First National Bank of Eureka Springs, Arkansas circa 1920s. Courtesy Eureka Springs Historical Museum.

bank. Also present in the financial institution were several customers later identified as Robert and John Easley along with Luther Wilson and John Holland.

Charlie Price, positioning himself in the center of the lobby, loudly proclaimed "Hands up, this is a robbery!" prior to ordering the crowd of bank employees and witnesses to move towards the back wall with their hands in the air. Unfortunately for the bandits, Cashier Smith paused a split second before obeying the bandit's command

Safe, First National Bank Of Eureka Springs. Courtesy Eureka Springs Historical Museum.

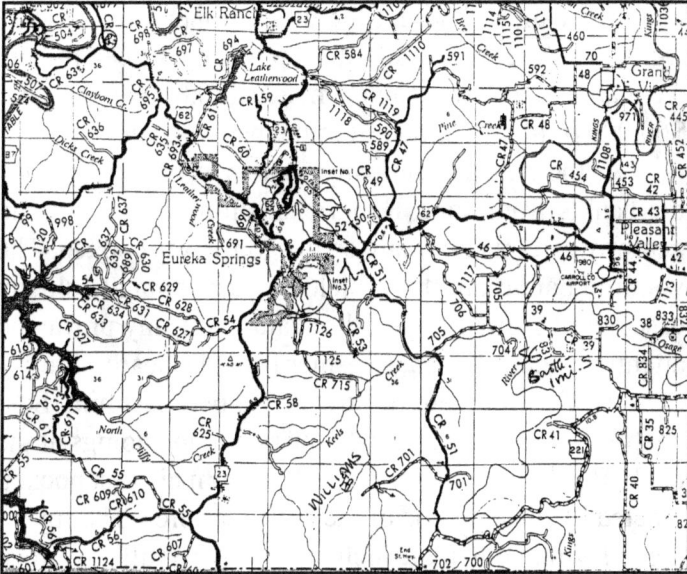

Map of Eureka Springs, Arkansas area. Courtesy Eureka Springs Historical Museum.

in order to stomp on the silent alarm, which was connected to the telephone exchange at the Basin Spring Hotel and several other locations about town. Within minutes, a crowd of citizens began piling out of their places of business throughout the downtown area. Most of the townsfolk, having been previously instructed on how to respond to hearing the bank's alarm, were armed to the teeth.

Meanwhile, just down the street at the Basin Spring Hotel a desk clerk and World War vet named Robert Bowman decided to investigate the commotion. After cramming a .45 caliber pistol into his back pocket, he and a pal, Claude Arbuckle, rushed to the First National and strolled into the lobby where they were met by the outstretched gun barrels of John Cowan and Si Wilson who ordered the duo to join the gaggle of hostages who had been since shoved into the counting room. The pair, realizing the bandits had got the drop on them, did as they were told. After this brief interruption, the Price brothers went about harvesting an estimated $10,000 in cash and $60,000 in liberty bonds from the bank's coffers.

As the crowd of curiosity seekers warily approached the bank's front door, Hendricks, sitting in the running getaway car, quickly realized his goose was cooked. The youthful bandit put the vehicle in gear hoping to slowly ease out of harm's way without attracting any unwanted attention. Glen Burson, a cashier from the nearby Eureka State Bank, observed the strange rig pull past him. Suspecting the driver was somehow tied to the doings at the bank, Burson, producing a revolver from his vest pocket, reacted by blasting one of the car's rear tires. The rig careened wildly down the incline traveling a full city block before crashing into a utility pole located across from the Basin Spring Park. Hendricks, gripped with fear, bailed out of the stopped vehicle and started running down the hilly street. Jess Littrell, who operated a nearby popcorn stand, and Sam Harmon, a taxi driver, who were both armed with shotguns, began chasing the boy, ordering him to stop. The fleeing youth's only response was to turn on the speed. Seeing a large curb directly in front of him, Hendricks attempted to leap over the obstacle but failed hitting the concrete with a thud. On rising from his fall, he was greeted with a volley of shots. After being struck in the right shoulder and face by a load of birdshot, he began pleading with his tormentors to cease-fire. After his surrender, the wounded lad was reportedly hog-tied and placed on a nearby park bench.

Meanwhile, back in the bank, the rest of the gang, failing to hear the commotion outside, completed the robbery and after peering out the front door noticing the crowd of rubberneckers, Charlie Price, ordered Bankers Smith and Sawyer to accompany them to their vehicle for use as human shields. On reaching the sidewalk, Smith suddenly jerked loose of Price's firm grip. Sawyer followed suit and both men flung themselves to the sidewalk hugging the hot concrete. Confronted by an empty space where their getaway car had been parked and the hostile crowd of armed citizens who had mostly taken cover in defensive positions, the four bandits stood momentarily in the middle of the street looking like deer caught in the headlights. Witnesses reported George Price turned to his brother saying, "They got us trapped. We will all be killed." Charlie Price, realizing escape by vehicle was no longer an option, pointed toward a narrow stone staircase located directly across the road from the bank lodged between Crows Bakery and the newspaper office. The staircase led to a lower street level (Center Street) and possible freedom. The two brothers took the lead scampering toward the stairs while Cowan followed a few feet behind them and Wilson brought up the rear.

Inside the bank, Bob Bowman, realizing the bandits had left the building, jerked out his pistol which he had hidden deep in his rear pocket and approached the front door. When he observed the hostages fall to the pavement, he took advantage of the situation firing six rounds through the closed screen door. Four bullets lodged in the side of a telephone pole located across the street while the fifth struck Si Wilson in the shoulder and the final missile hitting John Cowan in the foot. (When the round was dug out of Cowan later that day, wire mesh from the screen door was found imbedded deep in the wound)

At the same time as the nervy hotel clerk was ambushing the bandits, Joe McKimmey, an attorney and former combat soldier, took notice of the happenings in the street from his office window located on the second floor of the bank building which overlooked the front door of the financial institution. Grabbing a .38 caliber pistol from his desk drawer, the attorney rushed to the open window cutting loose with a volley of rounds, several which struck the wounded Wilson in his exposed backside. In the meantime, Ernie Jordan, who operated a nearby jewelry shop, grabbed his pistol and dashed into the street. Kneeling down on one knee, he calmly fired several hot lead projectiles into the chest of the dying bandit. Wilson, struck by eight bullets, whirled around facing his tormentors, fired one round that nicked the right side of Jordan's face, and with a look of shock on his face fell dead in his tracks.

Emerging from the sidelines, Constable Homer Brittain, armed with a pair of .38's, joined the fray. Positioning himself in a gunman's stance the constable began firing both pistols simultaneously. While Charlie Price and Cowan fled down the open stairwell, George Price, who was carrying a canvas bag containing the loot, suddenly whirled about facing Brittain and engaged the lawman in a fierce old-west style gun-duel. After trading nearly a dozen shots, Price suddenly gripped his chest, violently falling headfirst down the stairs, his body ending up draped over a stair railing hanging suspended in midair. The bag containing the loot fell aimlessly down the stone steps bouncing onto the edge of Center Street.

Meanwhile, Charlie Price, already hit twice by fire coming from a pair of citizens shooting from an open window across the street, and his companion Cowan dragging his crippled foot, attempted to reach the bottom of the concrete stairwell. The pair was abruptly hit with a cascade of rounds fired from a group of citizens who had joined Constable Brittain and Ernie Jordan at the top of the stairs. Turning toward his antagonists, Charlie reportedly fired several rounds with his pistol before falling headfirst down the stairs, his body coming to rest against a lamppost. Cowen, struck by a round in the right leg just above his knee, slumped to the pavement about midway down the steps. Begging the posse men to stop firing, he slung his revolver away and surrendered. Charlie Price, gut-shot and in great pain, slowly lifted his head and began pleading for a drink of water. Just ten minutes after the robbery had began it ended. The parties involved had fired an estimated fifty rounds. According to witnesses, the stairway looked like a slaughterhouse.

Moments after the firing died down, with gunpowder still drifting in a smoky haze over the battlefield, Homer Brittain approached a prostrate George Price asking him his name. The bandit, speaking in a whisper, halt-

Modern day view of the stairwell where the bandits made their last stand. Photo by Naomi Morgan.

Citizen defenders, Eureka Springs bamk raid. Courtesy Eureka Springs Historical Museum.

ingly replied, "Take me to a hospital and I will tell you all." A dozen volunteers began carrying the wounded robbers up the stairs placing them in several waiting automobiles to be transported to the nearby Huntington Hos-

Armed citizens standing next to wrecked car that was driven by Mark Hendricks. Courtesy Eureka Springs Historical Museum.

Basin Spring, near where the bandit's car wrecked, above is Southern Hotel where Price and Wilson allegedly played cards the day before the failed holdup. Courtesy Eureka Springs Historical Museum.

Name _Wilson, Si_
Blk _Potter's Field_
Lot _____
Plot _____
Date of Death _27 September 1922_
Date of Burial _____
Purchaser _____
Funeral Director _____

I.O.O.F. book – no information. No card in file.

Killed while attempting to rob First National Bank.

Body unclaimed by any relative. Believe to be native of OKLAHOMA

Cemetery record for Si Wilson. Courtesy Eureka Springs Historical Museum.

pital. Si Wilson, dead on the scene, was moved to the Blocksom Funeral Parlor. George Price was pronounced dead within minutes of his arrival at the hospital. Charlie Price was stabilized then taken to surgery. Cowan was also operated on, a bullet was extracted from his foot and his broken leg set. A dozen birdshot pellets were plucked from the hide of young Hendricks. A nurse told the local newspaper the youth had babbled in a foreign tongue (Cherokee) while on the operating table.

Back at the scene of the gunfight, confusion reined. Souvenir hunters swept the area for bullet casings, and pried spent rounds out of the wood-work of the adjacent buildings. At the site of the disabled getaway car,

Posse member Ernest Jordan and an unidentified individual. Courtesy Eureka Springs Historical Museum.

folks picked up debris and broken glass from the wreck and cut pieces off the damaged wooden utility pole. (Incidentally, the getaway car's license plates were discovered attached to the frame upside down, obviously in hopes of thwarting witnesses from being able to read it correctly).

A photographer named Gray assembled the posse and numerous other citizens for a series of group pictures. At the funeral home, Si Wilson's corpse was propped up and photos were taken of the body. Several hundred per-

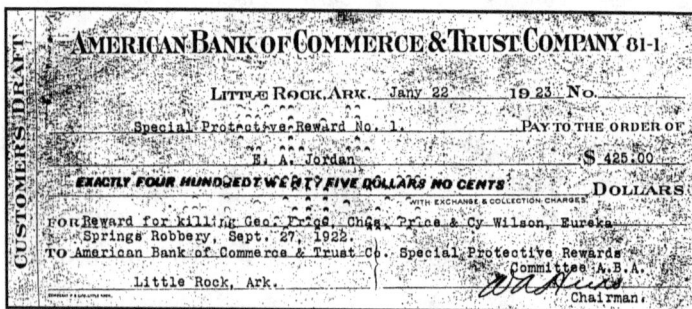

Cancelled check showing Ernest Jordan's part of the reward given by the Arkansas Bankers Association. Courtesy of the Eureka Springs Historical Museum.

Modern view showing bank, stairwell across street, and road Road leading down to spot where Hendricks wrecked the getaway car. Photo by Naomi Morgan.

sons milled up and down Spring Street asking questions of the posse members and gawking at the blood covered stairwell where the bandits made their last stand. The stolen bag of money was returned to bank President F.O. Butt. The handful of brave defenders who had fought the robbers to a standstill quickly became town heroes.

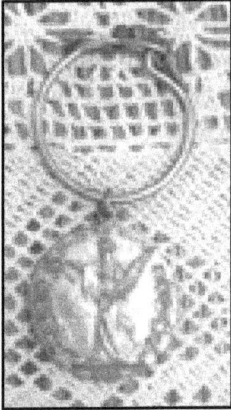

Medal of valor presented to Ernie Jordan by First National Bank after the robbery-on display at the Eureka Springs Historical Museum. Photo by Naomi Morgan.

That evening a reporter interviewed the wounded bandits. Young Mark Hendricks told the newsman he had never been involved in a crime before and had joined up with his fellow robbers only a few days ago at the Cookson, Oklahoma home of George Price. When asked if he was part Indian he answered in the affirmative. When the newsman visited Charlie Price he was unconscious, but the nurses at his side stated he had called out, "Let's go to Eureka Springs boys" repeatedly while under anesthesia.

While the reporter was visiting John Cowan, the wounded outlaw stated "I have known the Price boys for years and lived near George." Adding, "I did not know Hendricks's name until you informed me of it." He also told the journalist he was currently growing twenty acres of cotton on shares back in Cookson and needed to tend his field. The middle-aged bandit then clammed up, claiming he felt poorly and didn't feel like talking.

Later that night, a sleepless Ernest Jordan, the lone injured member of the posse who had participated in the gun battle with the bad men, came to the hospital in agony.

Evidently, the bullet fired by Si Wilson, which narrowly missed his head by a millimeter, had left a trail of gunpowder burns on his face and in his eyes. Although the injury had gone virtually unnoticed by him during the past ten hours, probably due to the day's excitement and the accompanying adrenaline rush, his eyes were now burning fiercely and wracked with pain.

The afternoon following the robbery, Charlie Price's three sisters arrived in town escorted by Sequoyah County Sheriff C. M. Gay. After taking rooms at the Allen Cottage, the women, who all had reputations as respectable folk back in Sallisaw, visited their sibling who was still unconscious.

Sheriff Gay, after consulting with Carroll County Sheriff Ed McShane talked to reporters. He announced he had been informed that an individual who knew him on sight had spotted the notorious Ed Lockhart, who was an associate of the Price brothers, near the bandit's campsite the day before the robbery. Gay expressed an opinion in which he pointed the finger at Lockhart as the mastermind behind the botched robbery.

The following day, Sheriff McShane told the editor of the Eureka Springs newspaper that several reliable witnesses had seen a partner of Lockhart's, Jack Jackson, who was currently out on bond for suspicion of robbing the Hulbert, Oklahoma bank, and an unnamed individual motoring

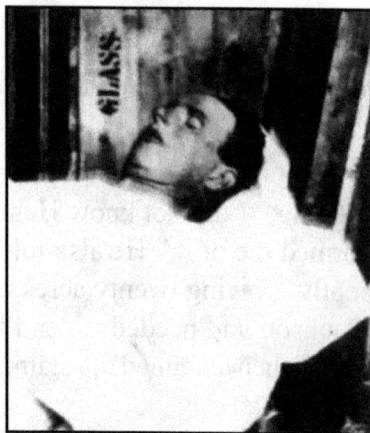

Si Wilson in death. Courtesy Eureka Springs Historical Museum.

through town in a Ford Coup the day after the failed bank heist. Putting two and two together the lawman suggested Lockhart and Jackson were probably sitting at an undisclosed location acting as scouts and backup to the other robbers at the time of the assault on the bank. Since the Cookson Gang had often used a backup car in their robberies in the past, and the Ford Coupe Wilson was driving when he met with his companions at their Leatherwood Creek campground had not yet been accounted for, this assumption holds a great deal of validity.

While one of the Price sisters accompanied George's body back to Sallisaw where he was buried at the Buffington Cemetery, the other two remained at Charlie's bedside. Although several area newspapers ran articles suggesting Charlie Price never regained consciousness, the Muskogee Times-Democrat, reported he made a deathbed confession in the presence of a small group of officials and citizens on the evening of September 30. In his statement, the outlaw purportedly admitted his and his brother's (Reece) complicity in the robbery of the bank of Muldrow. As for the missing $15,000 in negotiable Liberty Bonds stolen from the Muldrow bank, he remained silent. When asked how he had gotten started down his road to destruction, he admitted his older brother Reece had enticed him and his other siblings into the business beginning with an unnamed Arkansas bank robbery. In response to being asked what went wrong in the Eureka robbery. Charlie responded, "He (Hendricks) drove off in the getaway car, but I don't blame him, he's just a boy," adding, "They have me charged with stealing thousands of dollars from other banks as well. I guess the surest way to beat 'em all is to die." Charlie passed away the following morning. Witnesses, who were by his side at the end, claimed the twenty-nine-year-old outlaw had "died game."

Four days after the debacle in Eureka Springs, the plain wooden coffin containing the remains of Charlie Price was moved by rail in the company of his sisters to Sallisaw where he was laid to rest a few feet from his brother on October 3. The flamboyant outlaw was provided military honors due to his service in the Great War. Before leaving Eureka Springs, the sisters made a statement to the local press, expressing their appreciation for the kindness shown them by the area's citizens and stating their lack of ill will toward the town for the deaths of their brothers.

Grave of Charlie Price. Photo by Naomi Morgan.

Si Wilson, whose body went unclaimed, was buried in an unmarked pauper's grave at the Odd Fellows Cemetery in Eureka Springs.

On October 15, the Oklahoma and Arkansas Banker's Association forked over $3000 in reward money to be evenly divided between a half-dozen of the Eureka Springs defenders. The same individuals were also presented small medallions or medals by the bank to commemorate their acts of bravery.

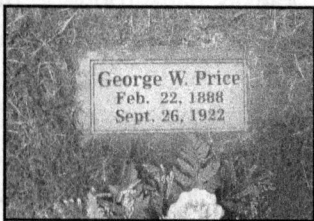
Grave of George Price, date of death is incorrect, should read September 27. Photo by Naomi Morgan.

In the days following the robbery, newspapers

throughout the nation noted the event with bold headlines applauding the town's defenders and comparing the raid to the catastrophe that had befallen the Dalton brothers in Coffeyville, Kansas three decades past.

In the days and weeks following the shootout, the notion of the Eureka Springs raid being a designed setup began to take root among the general populace of Eastern Oklahoma. In the aftermath of the robbery a story sprang up, which suggested the robbers had meant to rob the bank at exactly noon, when banks were usually vacant and the streets empty due to it being the lunch hour. The tale went on to claim Charlie Price had forgotten to wind his timepiece, consequently causing the gang to launch the raid an hour ahead of sched-

Top: John Cowan
Bottom: Marcus Hendricks
The only two bandits to survive the shootout in the Eureka Springs bank robbery attempt. Photo courtesy of the Eureka Springs Historical Society.

ule, thus thwarting the raiders from making a clean getaway. Many Cookson Hill residents scoffed at the so-called faulty timepiece theory, claiming the story was a fabrication invented to protect the identity of an informant. Although, at first glance one must admit the shootout appeared more like a prearranged ambush than a spur of the moment affair, there is little or no existing evidence to back up this theory.

Artie Pendergrass.
Courtesy Arkansas
Gazette.

Several months after the Eureka Springs robbery, a quartet of masked bandits raided the Farmers and Merchants Bank of Mountain Home, Arkansas, looting the institution of several thousand dollars in cash and $1550 in Liberty Bonds. Lawmen immediately suspected the robbery was the work of Ed and Sam Lockhart along with a crime partner named Artie Pendergrass and his son.

On January 12, 1923, Pinkerton detectives announced the arrest of the long missing 'Tump" Price in California. It appears the youngest of the Price boys had fled the "Sooner" state sometime in the spring of 1922. Pinkerton operatives, acting on behalf of the Oklahoma Banker's Association, tracked him across the country, capturing the elusive fugitive as he was exiting a rooming house in San Francisco's Russian Hill District. Price was extradited back to Tahlequah, Oklahoma on January 18, 1923 and charged with participating in the ransacking of the Hulbert bank.

Within days of his arrival back in Oklahoma, young Price confessed to Cherokee County prosecutors that he and his deceased brothers, George, and Charlie, along with the assistance of a nameless individual had indeed robbed the Hulbert bank. When quizzed if either Fred Walker or Ed Lockhart played any role in the robbery, the youthful outlaw claimed they had not. Contradicting "Tump's" statement was the testimony of the Hulbert bank clerk who had positively identified Lockhart as being present at the event, as well as Lewis Curtis's convoluted confession that also placed the elusive bandit at the scene.

Judgment document from Cherokee County Court for William Price. Courtesy Cherokee County Court Clerk.

On February 28, 1923, twenty-six-year-old William Price was sentenced to five years hard labor in the Oklahoma State Penitentiary. Although five other individuals had previously been charged with the Hulbert bank raid, young Will Price would go down in history as the only person ever convicted of the crime.

The day after "Tump's" day in court, John Cowan and Mark Hendricks stood before the bar of justice in Carroll County, Arkansas. Both men pled guilty to robbery. Due to Hendricks's tender age, the Judge sentenced him to only three years in prison but hammered Cowan, who was older and had a record, with a judgment of ten years at hard labor.

Chapter 8

Caught In the Act, Lockhart Takes a Powder, and a Killing in Ramona

In the early morning hours of February 20, 1923, Sallisaw, Oklahoma, night cop Perry Chuculate was making his rounds when he spotted a small light illuminating the garage of his brother-in-law, Sequoyah County Undersheriff Bert Cotton. Deciding to investigate, the officer was approaching the structure when suddenly he heard voices emitting from inside. Drawing his weapon, he carefully opened the garage door shining his flashlight into the near darkness. Seeing two men squatting next to Cotton's automobile, he cocked his revolver ordering the individuals to "freeze." Setting nearby was a five-gallon gasoline can and a siphoning hose. Upon searching the duo, Chuculate discovered both men were armed with .45 caliber automatic pistols. After handcuffing the pair, he contacted his brother-in-law requesting assistance. When the sleepy-eyed undersheriff began questioning the men, they became cagey and evasive. The older of the two identified himself as J. C. Henley, while the younger claimed his name was Matt Charlie. Suspecting the men were vagrants or hobos, the officers hauled them to the county lockup securing them behind bars. Cotton, thinking he noticed something familiar about one of the suspects, began studying a batch of wanted posters lying on his desk. Coming across a flyer relating to the notorious Ed

Lockhart, the lawman cried "Eureka!" when he noticed the photo on the poster perfectly matched one of the prisoners. On further questioning, the suspects admitted their identities. Lockhart, who had been holed-up in the Arkansas hills since his escape from the Boone County jail the previous year, represented a big catch for the officers, a proverbial "feather in their caps." The outlaw was wanted for a host of crimes in a wide area, including the robberies of the banks of Gore and Hulbert, Oklahoma, as well as those in Harrison and Mountain Home, Arkansas, and Seligman, Missouri, along with jail escape, horse and auto theft. After further interrogation, Lockhart's young companion admitted his name was Thomas "Kie" Carlile, a wayward Cherokee County youth who was wanted in connection with several area auto thefts. Incidentally, Carlile was Mount Cookson's brother-in-law.

Since the pair was obviously attempting to steal a

Officers Perry Chuculate, left and Bert Cotton on horseback. Courtesy Sequoyah County Historical Society.

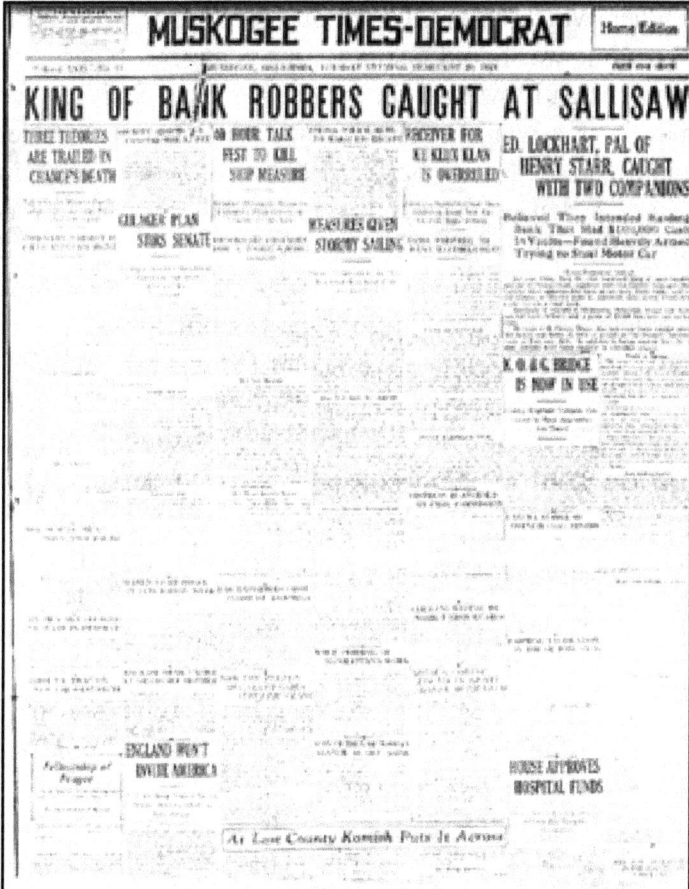

Headline in Muskogee Times-Democrat at the time of Lockhart's capture in Sallisaw.

quantity of gasoline at the time of their arrest, Cotton and Chuculate decided to tour the town looking for the suspects missing automobile. At dawn, the officers spotted a rickety Ford Roadster parked on the roadside just outside the city limits. Approaching the suspicious vehicle, Cotton noticed a young man napping in the front seat under a thin tattered blanket. Chuculate walked up to the half-open driver's side window thrusting a pistol into the individual's face, firmly calling for him to peaceably surrender, which he did. Under questioning, the driver admitted he was Sam Lockhart, Ed's younger brother, who was currently wanted for stealing a car in Sallisaw the past year, as well as being a suspect along with his older sibling in the November 28, 1922, raid on the Mountain Home, Arkansas, bank. Officers noted the car, which was in poor shape, was loaded down with rifles, shotguns, and a great deal of ammunition. It was later determined the vehicle had been stolen from the front of a residence in Boone County, Arkansas. The younger Lockhart promptly joined his notorious brother in the not so friendly confines of the Sequoyah County slammer. Sheriff John Johnson suspected the trio of having traveled to Sallisaw with the intent of robbing a local bank that had recently received a large shipment of cash. The day following the men's capture, officers arrested Charley White and charged him with harboring fugitives from justice. Apparently, Charley, who had been convicted of robbing the Park Hill bank but was currently on parole, had played host to the three suspects at his home in nearby

Ad placed in newspaper by the First National Bank of Sallisaw- circa 1923. Courtesy Sallisaw Democrat America.

Bunch the day before their capture. After being confined in the county lockup for a week White was released and the charges against him were eventually dropped.

While awaiting the suspects formal court hearings, Sheriff Johnson tightened up the jail's security measures and instructed his officers to began questioning any suspicious individuals arriving in town, proclaiming: "Lockhart's friends would not stop at anything to liberate him if they had half a chance."

Two days after the trio's arrest, jailors pulled a surprise inspection uncovering two knives and a hacksaw in Lockhart's cell. Later that day, a Sallisaw city policeman came across an elderly gentleman loitering in front of the jailhouse. When questioned, the seedy looking individual gave his name as George Hale. Upon searching the old man, the patrolman discovered a loaded .45 pistol and a razor sharp dagger stuffed in his pockets along with $79 hidden in a sock. After confiscating the pistol and knife, he admonished the character to move along. When describing the man's appearance to a pair of fellow officers at the station that evening, he was informed he just had an encounter with the one and only "Kaiser Bill" Goodman. The following day, Sallisaw officers corralled another suspicious acting individual who gave his name as J. E. Lowe of Tahlequah. After a short investigation it was discovered the man's real identity was Mack Moore of Sperry, Oklahoma, who it turns out was "Cotton" Walker's son-in-law and an associate of Ed Lockhart's. Moore was jailed overnight then released with the admonition to get out of town. Pronto!

As for the disposition of the primary suspects, "Kie" Carlile, who would one day achieve fame as one of the most active desperadoes of the depression era, was able to make bond, while Sam Lockhart was extradited to Arkansas to stand trial for the Mountain Home robbery.

When witnesses from the bank heist were unable to identify the bandit, Arkansas prosecutors reversed course, transporting him to Boone County where he was charged with stealing the car the pair of Oklahoma officers had discovered him snoozing in. Pleading guilty to the auto theft, Sam was sentenced to five years at the Tucker Prison Farm. Why he was not tried in Sallisaw for the September 1922 auto theft charge is a mystery.

With lawmen in both Harrison and Mountain Home demanding his extradition back to Arkansas, Ed Lockhart pled guilty to the December 1921 Gore, Oklahoma, bank robbery in order not to be extradited back to Arkansas, fearing the authorities would toss him into the Tucker farm where his little brother was heading. The 4,500-acre prison farm was noted for it's harsh living conditions and inhumane treatment of inmates. Prisoners were routinely whipped and tortured for the smallest infraction. Tucker, along with the Eastham Prison Farm in Texas, was reputably the nation's harshest penal farms in the 1920s and '30s

Appearance docket for Ed Lockhart and Jack Brodie on robbery charges. Courtesy Sequoyah County Clerk's office.

Knowing full well Lockhart was pleading guilty to the Gore job in order to avoid the horrors of Tucker, Judge J. H. Jarman chose to make an example of him. The jurist sentenced the outlaw to twenty years hard labor at the Oklahoma State Penitentiary, where he would join his pals "Cotton" Walker, Bush Wood, Mount Cookson, and Jack Brodie. On his arrival at the institution, which must have seemed like old home week to the bandit, prison officials described the thirty-three-year-old desperado as inmate #13052, five-foot eight-inches, 140 pounds, with black hair and a gold tooth, in addition to a prominent scar on his chin and a somewhat wasted appearance. It seems the bad man had picked up a dose of the prisoner's malady, tuberculosis, a common occurrence in the nation's over-crowded jails during the period. Apparently, he had contracted the dread disease while serving his stint in the Boone County jail in Harrison, Arkansas prior to his escape. Incidentally, when asked by prison officials what caused his downfall, the bandit responded, "hard times."

A few months after Lockhart's delivery to the state pen, Oklahoma's progressive Governor Jack Walton began passing out dozens of leaves of absence to any in-

Appearance docket for Ed Lockhart and Brodie on horse larceny charges. Courtesy Sequoyah County Clerk's office.

Main gate, Tucker Prison Farm, Arkansas circa 1929. Courtesy Arkansas Department of Corrections.

mate with a good sob story. Lockhart, knowing a good thing when he saw it, quickly made application to the state's Chief Executive for a hardship release claiming his family was currently in a state of extreme poverty. Amazingly, he was granted a six-month leave of absence on August 21, 1923, after serving only a few months of his sentence. Bush Wood, who had been convicted for the 1921 Locust Grove robbery, would also be a recipient of one of these "get out of jail free" passes. In hindsight, Governor Walton's attempts at prison reform and his program of compassionate leaves proved to be a dismal failure. According to a prison spokesman, Lockhart had agreed to take over his father's (who had recently died) farm near Sallisaw to earn his daily bread. Ironically, the actual title to the farm was in the hands of a large land holding company, which had on its board of directors none other than recently reelected Congressman W. W. Hastings, who had been the lead prosecutor in the recent Park Hill and Hulbert robbery cases. When this bit of information hit the newspapers, Hastings, embarrassed by

Lockhart's prison login sheet dated 4-10-23. Courtesy Kenneth Butler and the Oklahoma Department of Corrections.

the revelation, publicly denied any affiliation with Lockhart or his family.

The day after the outlaw gained his freedom, two unmasked men robbed the Southern State Bank of Maize, Oklahoma, located twenty-five miles due north of

Muskogee. After looting the institution of $1644, the bandits kidnapped bank teller J. C. McGuinn and a customer forcing the pair to ride on the running boards of their getaway car for eight miles before releasing them. A garage operator who witnessed the bandits force the hostages on to their car phoned the county sheriff's office in Pryor. Responding to the emergency, Mayes County Sheriff J. A. Layton and a deputy took off in their Ford Model "T" Police Cruiser toward the scene of the crime. A few miles south of Claremore, the officers briefly caught sight of the fugitive's fleeing "Marmon" automobile, but never got within shooting range of the speeding flivver. After a thirty-minute "high-speed" chase, (bear in mind a Model "T's" top speed was only forty-five miles per hour downhill) the lawmen abandoned their pursuit of the bandits near the community of Bushyhead.

Oklahoma Governor Jack Walton. Author's private collection.

Later that day, the owner of a hardware store in Maize came forward stating he had sold a quantity of ammunition to two well-dressed men who fit the description of the bandits, only moments before the bank robbery. A report was later received from Claremore stating a car matching the description of the getaway vehicle had been stolen earlier that morning from a commercial garage. Apparently, the fugitives had forced an employee of the garage at gunpoint to fill the car with gas before taking him hostage. After driving six miles west of Claremore, one of the men physically threw the man out of the moving car onto a gravel road. Luckily, the poor fellow suffered only few bumps and bruises from the harrowing experience. When interviewed by police he stated the hijackers were drinking heavily. In response to the robbery, a dozen roadblocks manned by lawmen armed with riot shotguns were set up along the roadways leading from Oklahoma into Kansas and Missouri.

Suspicion of pulling off the Maize job was immediately attached to Lockhart due to his being seen in nearby Muskogee the morning of the robbery. Under pressure from several dozen-area lawmen and his political enemies, Governor J. C. Walton immediately cancelled Lockhart's leave of absence and issued a warrant for his arrest. On receipt of the warrant, Sequoyah County Sheriff John Johnson and half-dozen deputies raided the home of Lockhart's brother-in-law near McKey, but come up empty.

Ten days after the Maize bank heist, a pair of individuals was arrested in Sioux City, Iowa driving the getaway car (minus any license plates) and in possession of most of the stolen loot from the robbery along with several loaded revolvers. One of the suspects was identified as Frank Rucker Jr. of nearby Claremore while the other was Lockhart's old crime partner, Rufus Rollen, who had participated with Lockhart, Henry Starr, and Charley

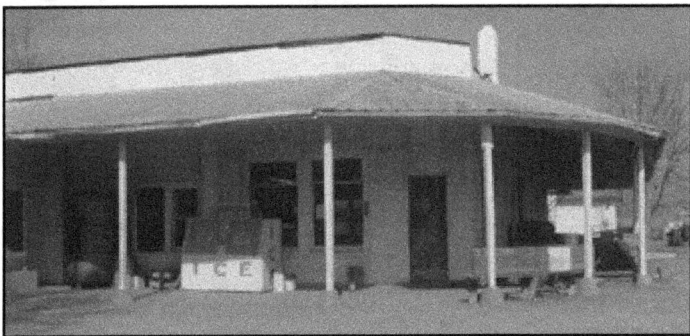

Maize, Oklahoma, today. Photo by Naomi Morgan.

Brackett in the 1921 Harrison, Arkansas bank robbery. Rufus had recently been paroled from the Arkansas Prison System, where he was serving a three-year term for his part in the Harrison bank raid. After several days of intense questioning, the pair was extradited back to Mayes County, Oklahoma to face the music. Although Rucker promptly pled guilty and was sentenced to twenty-five years in the pen, Rollen denied any involvement in the crime, claiming he had accompanied Rucker to Iowa just to be along for the ride. It appears he may have been telling the truth. The following month a man named Bill Trotter was arrested and confessed to being Rucker's accomplice in the robbery. Although the authorities were still convinced Rollen had some culpability in the bank heist, they were forced to release him from custody.

Upon learning of his newfound status as a fugitive, Lockhart, who had spent the first few days after his release in the company of his wife at a hotel in Muskogee, packed his bags and fled the area. He soon hooked up with Berry Dotson's son, Bee, who was currently "scouting" on an auto-theft charge. The pair reportedly sought refuge from the law in a rugged section of the Cookson Hills southeast of Barber, Oklahoma (now the Cookson Hills Wildlife Management Area).

On the evening of September 15, Cherokee County Deputy Sheriff Jim "Soggy" Sanders received a call informing him of an abandoned car parked on an isolated road near the community of Wauhillau. Arriving at the scene, Sanders began surveying the automobile seeking clues to its ownership. Suddenly he heard the voice of a man ordering him to "Get em up, pal." He turned and observed Ed Lockhart, who he knew by sight, and Bee Dotson holding pistols aimed at his midsection. The lawmen did as he was told. The pair of desperadoes proceeded to steal the officer's gun, wallet, and hat. To add insult to

Court document charging Frank Rucker Jr. and Rufus Rollen (misspelled in document) with armed robbery of Maize, Oklahoma bank. Courtesy of Mayes County Court Clerk.

Mayes County Sheriff J. A. Layton. Courtesy of Mayes County Sheriff's Department.

injury, the hijackers informed the frustrated deputy they were swapping cars with him, saying they were "trading up." Sanders then observed the pair abandon their broken down Model "T" "rust bucket" on the roadside before fleeing the scene in his late model Ford Touring car.

On the morning of October 4, Delaware County Sheriff Ben Smith received a phone call from one of his "stool pigeons" informing him of unusual activity on the farm of a local "character" named Pete Baker, which was located near the village of Leach, Oklahoma. The caller went on to state, he had seen numerous new or nearly new vehicles come and go from the farm in the past few days. He also claimed, when he visited Baker earlier that morning for the purpose of borrowing some fence wire, he overheard a young man address an older companion as "Nash". The mention of the name Nash immediately got the Sheriff's juices up due to a nationwide search presently underway for three men who had robbed the KATY railroad express car near Okesa, Oklahoma, on August 18, 1923 of several

Jim "Soggy" Sanders. Courtesy Cherokee County Sheriff's Department.

Headlines Muskogee Times-Democrat, *October 9, 1923.*

thousand dollars in Liberty Bonds. The leader of the trio was known to have been the infamous Al Spencer who had recently been slain by lawmen near Bartlesville, and his companions, Grover Durrull and Frank "Jelly" Nash. When asked to describe the older man the youth had addressed as Nash, the snitch gave a description that closely matched that of the fugitive train robber. Smith instructed the informant to keep an eye on the farm while he formed

---

a plan of action. The Sheriff immediately contacted Federal Marshal Bill Meeks in Vinita before rounding-up a posse that consisted of Deputies Jack Carey, Grover Munroe, Charles Rowe, George Squirrel, and Red Booth. On the arrival of Marshal Meeks, the party of officers drove out to the informant's residence, which was located near Baker's farm.

At roughly the midnight hour, the posse approached the Baker farm on foot walking up a wooded draw. Five of the men led by Marshal Meeks surrounded the home while Sheriff Smith and Deputy Carey began searching the out buildings. After breaking down both the front and back doors with heavy sledgehammers, the officers poured into the residence, guns drawn. Baker, who was sitting at the dining room table playing solitaire and nipping on a jug of home brew, meekly lifted his hands in surrender. No one else was found in the home. While searching the barn, Sheriff Smith and his companion heard a loud snor-

Delaware County Sheriff Ben F. Smith, left, and Deputies Henry Rogers and George Hogan, circa 1920s. Courtesy Delaware County Historical Museum.

ing sound in the hayloft. When they peered in, they discovered two sleeping men, who according to the lawmen were dressed in bib-overalls. The pair of lawmen reacted to their find by sticking the barrel of a .12 gauge shotgun and a large caliber handgun into the suspect's faces. The pair of slumbering individuals, who were both armed with government .45s, raised their hands in submission realizing the gig was up. A search of the premises turned up a whiskey still, two stolen cars, and an arsenal of guns.

Frank "Jelly" Nash.
Courtesy Okmulgee Daily Times.

Shortly after the raid, the three-manacled prisoners were removed to the Delaware County jail in nearby Jay for questioning. After undergoing a vigorous session of interrogation, the two mysterious suspects who had been apprehended in the barn identified themselves as Berry Dotson and none other than the widely sought Ed Lockhart. Although the identification of Lockhart came as a surprise to the lawmen, they were elated to have the celebrated bandit in their custody. Unfortunately for the officers, the young man who had been visiting the trio at Baker's farm earlier in the day and had reportedly referred to one of the men as "Nash," was no where to be found. Marshal Meeks, convinced the man calling himself Dotson was in reality "Jelly" Nash, had the prisoner transported to the Federal jail in Vinita and held for suspicion of train robbery. After several witnesses who knew Nash by sight were unable to identify the suspect, Dotson was released from Federal custody into the waiting arms of Mayes County officials who charged him with auto theft, due to two of the cars found in the raid on Baker's farm having recently been reported as stolen off the busy streets of nearby Tulsa. Dotson was able to make bond on the charges the following day.

Although officials at the Oklahoma state pen were notified of Lockhart's capture, there was a slight delay in picking up and transporting the fugitive back to the "big house" due to a paper work snafu. It turned out to be a costly error on the part of the authorities. The following morning, the outlaw was photographed and processed. On looking at his freshly taken likeness, the bandit informed his captors, "That's a damn good picture." Baker was also processed and held on manufacturing illegal whiskey and vehicle theft charges.

On the evening of October 7, at roughly half past seven, five masked men burst into the Delaware County jail armed with pistols and rifles. Deputy Jack Carey who was the only officer on duty at the time, was sitting at a desk shooting the breeze with a friend, Perry Author, when he observed the invaders rush into the jail's main lobby led by a youth waving a pistol who ordered the jailor and

Delaware County jail. Courtesy Delaware County Historical Museum.

his companion to "Put em up." Taken unaware, the pair complied with the raider's demands. Relieving Carey of his gun and jail keys, the youth, who despite his tender age, appeared to be in charge, strolled into the cell area where he informed Lockhart, who was hurriedly dressing, to "Put on your pants Ed, you're out of here." The young man also told Lockhart's fellow inmates, "If any of you boys are coming with us, throw away your hats, we only want fighting men." Even though the inmate

Headlines of jailbreak. Courtesy Muskogee Times-Democrat.

population in the jail was made up of several desperate characters including the recently arrested Carl Reasoner, a former member of Al Spencer's band of brigands, no one took the boy up on his offer. The invaders locked the deputy and his buddy into Lockhart's now empty cell before turning on their heels fleeing into the darkness.

Evidently, the door to the cell the two victims had been forced into had not fully locked, allowing them to quickly escape from their brief captivity and give the alarm. A BOLO (be on the lookout) was issued to law enforcement agencies throughout a three state area within minutes of the jail raid. After studying a mass of collected mug shots, Jailor Carey and his companion were able to identify three of the invaders as the recently paroled Bush Wood, as well as Bee Dotson and his seventeen-year-old brother, Charley, who had been the young spokesman for the group. When Sheriff Smith requested background information on Charley Dotson from the authorities in Muskogee, he was informed the lad had recently been arrested and released on charges stemming from a whiskey violation in their fair city. After looking at Charley's mug shot, the informant from the Baker farm raid identified him as the youth he had seen at the farm prior to the raid.

Just forty-eight hours after the jail delivery a posse consisting of a dozen officers crossed paths with Lockhart and several companions near the Cherokee County village of Pettit. After exchanging two-dozen shots in a hot gun-duel with the lawmen, the fugitives, abandoning their car, somehow managed to slip away on foot melting into the heavily timbered hills. Amazingly, no one was hit by any of the many rounds fired in the incident. Although scores of area lawmen and armed volunteers conducted a frantic search for the desperate band of fugitives over the next few days, no sign was found of the raiders. Sequoyah

County Sheriff John Johnson and a handpicked posse again searched the homes of Lockhart's relatives near the communities of Marble City and McKey, Oklahoma, but like their cohorts in Cherokee County, they met no success. Arkansas lawmen in turn raided the bad man's haunts in Searcy County, but they too hit a dry hole.

Less than a week after the jailbreak, Lockhart, along with Bush Wood and Charley Dotson, were spotted in a crowded pool hall on Garrison Avenue in downtown Fort Smith, Arkansas. Witnesses described the trio as loud and drinking heavily. Somehow becoming aware of the danger, the trio suddenly departed the gin mill just moments before the arrival of police. An hour later, the fugitives were sighted motoring through nearby Van Buren. Officers rushed to the area, but once again found no trace of the fleeing outlaws. The following day, the automobile the suspects were using was found abandoned on the roadside near Stilwell, Oklahoma. On the evening of October 13, Fort Smith detectives captured Bee Dotson and a man named Pete Shaves in a rundown rooming house located in the city's midtown district. According to news reports, the men were in the company of a pair of "ladies" who were described by reporters as being "real tomatoes" at the time of their arrest. Both men were quickly extradited from Arkansas back to Jay, Oklahoma where they posted heavy bonds and were released from custody. Dotson promptly "took a powder" fleeing to parts unknown. A warrant was issued for his rearrest.

It appears the motivation for all the hyper police and vigilante cooperation in the effort to capture Lockhart and his associates seems to have been at least partially spurred by the fact that a combined $6000 reward for Lockhart's arrest had been issued from both the Arkansas and Oklahoma Banker's Association the day after his escape from the Jay jail.

On November 14, 1923, news was received of Lockhart's ex-partner in crime, "Cotton" Walker. It seems the slippery outlaw who was serving a twelve-year stretch at McAlester prison, had been working in the prison tobacco factory when he noticed the guard assigned to his crew was sound asleep in his chair. Walker, taking advantage of this opportunity, slipped out an unguarded exit and began strolling towards town. On arriving at the railyards, he hopped into an empty boxcar riding it to Texas where he had friends who provided him sanctuary.

A week after Walker's escape, Bee Dotson was recaptured at his father's residence near Ramona, Oklahoma. He was charged with jumping bail on the jail delivery charge as well as auto-theft (stealing Deputy Sanders car as well as others) and his alleged participation in a homicide that took place in Bartlesville earlier in the month. During the raid, the officer in charge, Ramona City Marshal J. P. Nicholson, allegedly abused the twenty-year-old Bee. When the boy's father, Berry, arrived the following day at the Bartlesville jailhouse where his son was being housed, he reportedly threatened Nicholson's life, saying, "I'm going to kill that G-d damn cop." A jailor who overheard the threat promptly arrested him. The forty-seven-year-old Dotson, who was currently on bond from an auto-theft charge as well as being wanted for questioning due to his suspected involvement with a bootlegging ring, soon joined his son in an adjoining cell. The following day, father and son were allowed to post a $5000 bond each, thus gaining their temporary freedom.

A week after his release from jail, Bee Dotson was called to testify in the Bartlesville murder case. Turns out, the lad had played no role in the murder in question, but lawmen insisted he had witnessed the event. Young Dotson took the stand but refused to answer the prosecutors pointed questions. The Ramona marshal who arrested the youth gave testimony in the case as to the character of Dotson. His statement, in which he called young Dotson "a thug of the first order," angered the boy's father who was attending the hearing. The elder Dotson reportedly left the courthouse again muttering threats on the life of the Ramona officer.

That evening, back in Ramona, the marshal was enjoying a relaxing game of billiards at the local pool hall when he looked up noticing an angry Berry Dotson approaching him. Dotson, who was known as a tough customer, abruptly smashed Nicholson square in the mouth, knocking him flat on his ass. When the marshal attempted to raise himself to his feet, Dotson, according to witnesses, caught him with a solid blow to the nose. Nicholson, bleeding profusely as the result of a cut lip and a broken nose, reacted by pulling his revolver and shooting his antagonist in the head, the round striking just above his attacker's right eye. Dotson's body reportedly pitched to the floor landing with a resounding thud. The mortally wounded outlaw was laid out on a nearby pool table where he lingered, barely alive, for less than two hours before expiring without regaining consciousness. The marshal de-

Modern day downtown Ramona, Oklahoma. Photo by Naomi Morgan.

Marshal Jim Nicholson.
Courtesy Rose Nicholson.

fended his actions by claiming Dotson was reaching for a gun when he shot him. When Dotson's body was searched at the McAllister Undertaking Parlor, he was found to be unarmed. That evening, young Bee Dotson arrived in Ramona with fire in his eyes and packing a rod. Friends of the marshal, knowing young Dotson would be seeking revenge for his father's death, whisked the injured officer to Bartlesville.

After a brief investigation, County Attorney C. F. Bailey charged Nicholson with murder. The lawman was allowed to post a $20,000 property bond before returning to his duties as Ramona Town Marshal.

At an inquest held several days later, Dotson's death was ruled a justifiable homicide and the charges against Marshal Nicholson dropped. The Judge noted it wasn't unreasonable for Nicholson to assume his life was in danger at the time of the assault due to Dotson's violent reputation and past threats on the lawman's life. On November 22, 1923, the body of Berry Dotson was laid to rest in a small cemetery located near his family's homestead at Dwight Mission, Oklahoma.

Chapter 9

The Death of a Bandit King

As the year 1923 rolled to an end, the manhunt for the elusive Ed Lockhart was proving to be an effort in futility. Although the tabloids reported numerous sightings of the bandit and one published account erroneously announced his capture in Springfield, Missouri, there were no substantiated sightings of the outlaw since he and his companions were seen exiting a Fort Smith poolroom in early October. There was even a questionable report of the bandit being arrested in early January 1924 and being lodged in the Shidler, Oklahoma town jail. The news flash went on to claim Lockhart had escaped custody a few days after his supposed incarceration. Other press releases speculated he was "scouting" in his old stomping grounds in either northern Arkansas or the Cookson Hills of Eastern Oklahoma.

In reality, the best evidence suggests the wily outlaw and his faithful minions (the Dotson brothers and probably Bush Wood) were plying their trade in the Osage "oil patch," an expansive area of oil field "boom" towns populated by thousands of well-paid roughnecks along with nearly as many "con men", hustlers, prostitutes, booze and dope peddlers, all vying to separate them from their hard earned wages. Due to the ongoing gas and petroleum boom, every one-horse village in the district was soon fitted out with some sort of banking institution in order to pay off oil-field workers and provide the busy

Oilfield workers, Oklahoma circa 1920s. Author's private collection.

cafés, dance halls, and stores a secure place to store their overflow of cash.

In late December, bandits struck the State Bank of Grainola, Oklahoma, located deep in the Osage Hills district. Lockhart's name was immediately placed on top of the suspect list. On January 2, 1924, the nearby First National Bank of Shidler, Oklahoma was robbed of an esti-

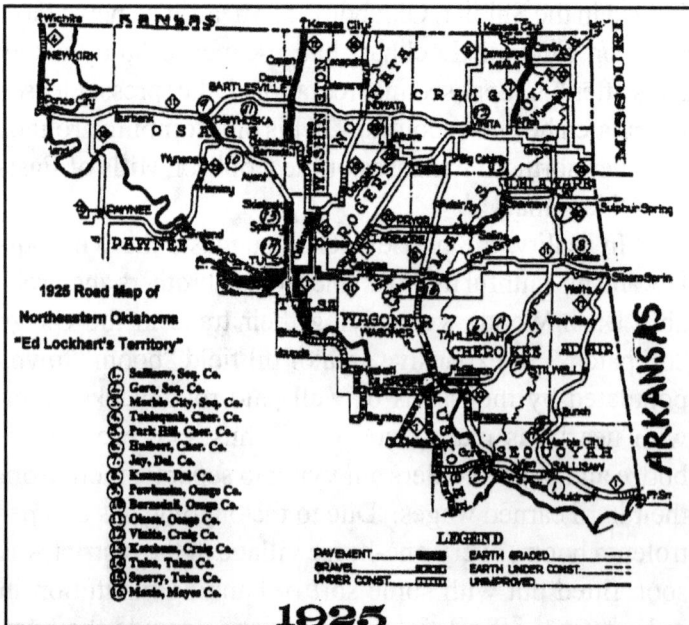

Ed Lockhart country. Courtesy Kenneth Butler.

Mont Grady, right, companion and prisoner. Courtesy The Muskogee Phoenix.

mated $8000 by two unmasked bandits. Although, Lockhart was initially branded as the chief culprit in the affair, the notorious Buster Jarrett and his sidekick Sam Coker were later charged with the robbery. Less than a month later, the same Shidler bank was struck again, being looted for nearly $2000 in cash and coin. This time, Lockhart was officially charged with the crime.

With $6600 in rewards offered for the capture of the desperado, dead or alive, Special Officer H. M. "Mont" Grady, who was employed by the Oklahoma state prison system as a full-time manhunter, devised a plan to trap the slick bandit. When he presented the prison's warden, William S. Keys, with his idea the chief keeper gave Grady and his scheme his full backing.

Grady, a half-blooded Choctaw Indian described as

a hard-living, hard-drinking hombre, had served a dozen years as a lawman. First as a guard at the Oklahoma State Pen, then a Muskogee city cop, and finally a Muskogee County deputy sheriff, before accepting his present position as a "hired gun" for the state. While serving as a Muskogee Deputy in 1921, Grady had participated in the capture of Lockhart's companion in the Harrison robbery, Rufus Rollen. Although, the steel-nerved lawman had slain several fugitives in his career, unlike many officers of the period, Grady was not noted as a man who "shot first and asked questions later."

The plan the manhunter presented the Warden was a simple one. It entailed a single man (Grady) devoting his every waking hour for a three-month period observing the movements of both Fred Walker and Lockhart's wives. Grady suspected the women were aiding the missing fugitives in their efforts to stay one step ahead of the law.

After only a month on the hunt, the lawman tracked

H. M. "Mont" Grady.
Courtesy Hartshorne Sun.

Tulsa County Sheriff Bob
Sanford. Courtesy Tulsa
County Sheriff's Department.

down the current whereabouts of Walker's wife who had disappeared around the time "Cotton" had escaped from the pen. It appears she had slipped away from her residence in the Cookson Hills moving to her daughter's isolated farmhouse located six miles west of the Osage Hills settlement of Sperry, Oklahoma. After spying on her residence for several days, Grady observed Fred Walker, Lockhart, and an unidentified man drive up to the residence staying only a few moments before departing. (The outlaw trio probably drove on to Lockhart's sister's farm in nearby Wildhorse) Unfortunately, Grady was alone at the time and did not possess the firepower needed to ambush the trio. When the lawman spotted an unaccompanied Lockhart drive up to the home in a Ford Coup the following night, Grady rushed back to nearby Tulsa recruiting the services of Tulsa County Sheriff Bob Sanford who quickly began assembling a posse made up of Deputies Jack Quast, J. E. Ferguson, Glenn Larkin, and Fred Murray.

At 5 am the next morning, the group of officers set out for the Walker farm in a single large Ford Touring car. On arriving in Sperry, Town Marshal Earl Maybe joined their ranks. At roughly 7 am, the posse, attempting to drive past the residence in question, got stuck in the mud directly in front of the home. Spotting Lockhart's Ford automobile still parked next to the residence, Sheriff Sanford ordered his deputies to bale out and surround the home on foot. Grady boldly volunteered to knock on the door in an effort to lure the bandit out in the open. Approaching the front entrance, he was met by Mrs. Fred Walker. While asking for directions to town, Grady spied Lockhart in the kitchen eating his breakfast. The bandit, looking up from his eggs, immediately recognized the lawman from the time he was an inmate and Grady a guard at the penitentiary.

The outlaw reacted by grabbing his high powered Savage rifle and in one giant leap, pounced on the lawman; leveling the gun's barrel directly in his chest saying, " Grady, stick 'em up." Walker's wife and young daughter, both standing nearby, immediately began pleading with the outlaw not to shoot the officer. In the meantime, Deputy Jack Quast, who had slipped behind the house, stepped into the back door aiming his rifle directly at the bandit's torso, saying," Give it up Ed." Lockhart responded by threatening to shoot Grady if Quast did not retreat out the door. Quast took note of the situation and slowly began withdrawing.

After disarming Grady of his .38 caliber pistol, which the outlaw stuffed into his trouser pocket, Lockhart slowly pushed the lawman out the front door and onto the dirt road using him as a human shield. Suddenly, Bob Sanford, who was hiding behind a nearby boulder, took a potshot at the pair, the round barely missing Grady's head. On hearing the whistle of the bullet as it flew past his ear, Grady called out to the Sheriff to cease-fire. Sanford, not

Headline Fort Smith, Arkansas, Southwest American *at time of Lockhart's death.*

"Still" Movie of How Lockhart Met Death

1 Special Officer Mont Grady enters door of house which had been surrounded by a sheriff's posse, and demands that Lockhart surrender. 2 Lockhart refuses, covering grady with his rifle, taking Grady's pistol and slipping it in the outside pocket of his coat. 3 Another officer enters the door and Lockhart shoves Grady in front of him as a shield, meanwhile forcing the other officer to withdraw. 4 Keeping Grady in front of him, Lockhart backs out the door retreating toward the woods, and continuing to use the officer as a shield. 5 As they near the woods, Lockhart raises his rifle and fires at the posse. Grady whirls, plunges his hand in Lockhart's pocket and fires the gun.

Cartoon strip depicting Lockhart's death. Courtesy Tulsa Daily World.

hearing his fellow officer's pleadings, took another pot-shot, which also missed the mark. Lockhart then fired a round at the lawman which also hit wide of it's the intended target. When the outlaw attempted to jack another round into the chamber of his rifle, Grady, seizing the opportunity, whirled around pushing the rifle barrel toward the ground with one hand while grabbing his own pistol, which was still jammed into Lockhart's pocket with the other. The lawman jerked the handgun's trigger firing one bullet that struck the outlaw in the midsection. Lockhart promptly fell face-first to the ground with an audible groan. Lying on the edge of the dirt road gasping for breath he was heard to let out a low moan then mutter: "My God, you've killed me." With that said, the desperado, in the throes of death, shuddered the full length of his body before lying still.

Shortly after the deadly shootout, Lockhart's remains were removed to the Mowbray Undertaking Parlors in nearby Tulsa. Sitting at a desk at the Tulsa County Sheriff's office, Mont Grady placed a call to his boss at the state pen in McAlester, telling him he'd got his man, explaining, "The son of a bitch took my gun, I had to kill him to get it back." That evening, a reporter from the Muskogee

Reward, headline Muskogee Daily Phoenix.

Phoenix interviewed a sleepless Grady at his east-side Muskogee home. The lawmen, in a pensive mood, summed up his feelings: "It was either him or me; I was convinced he intended on killing me. Every step I took with his rifle pointed at my spine I felt was a step closer to my grave. In the end, I got lucky, he didn't." He later added: "I kept a close eye on my pistol and may have been able to grab it in the house, but didn't want to start a battle in there endangering the women and children." Sitting in a corner of the room in plain sight was Lockhart's rifle and new snake hide "cowboy" boots, which Grady had snagged as souvenirs of his adventure. The following day the brave officer would receive by special post, the spent round he had fired into Lockhart's body ending the bad man's life. Grady, who was an honorable man, voluntarily split the huge reward with his fellow posse men. In the next few months, the manhunter became so popular with the local citizenry, a group of prominent businessmen asked him to run for Muskogee County Sheriff in the upcoming election. Although grateful for the offer, Grady declined the invitation.

Within hours of the desperado's death, several hundred morbidly curious sightseers began assembling at the mortuary demanding to get a look at the dead man. Seeing no harm in it, officials at the funeral home opened its doors to the public. Over the next forty-eight hours an estimated 1500 persons passed by the body, which was laid out in a cheap coffin. After waiting several days for the next of kin to show up and claim the body, Tulsa County officials began making plans to bury the outlaw in a potter's field. At the last moment, Lockhart's attractive wife, who lived in St. Joe, Arkansas made an appearance demanding local authorities put a stop to the flowing crowds pushing into the morgue, gawking at her husband's mortal remains. She also contacted the American Legion and VFW in Tulsa and Sallisaw, who after reviewing Lockhart's war record, agreed to help with the funeral expenses. A spokesman for the VFW explained, "Lockhart may have been a bad man as a civilian but he had been a good soldier."

The following day, March 31, 1924, the outlaw's body was transported by rail to Sallisaw where it was met by a crowd of several hundred persons on arrival at the Missouri-Pacific depot. The body was first taken to the American Legion headquarters in town where the coffin was opened for viewing. Within hours of the caskets arrival, an immense crowd of curiosity seekers besieged the building. The following morning, under a slate-gray sky, the family had the coffin transported by hearse to Lockhart's brother-in-law's farm near McKey where Reverend R. F. Thompson of the Sallisaw Presbyterian Church preached a private funeral. At 3 p.m., the remains were removed for internment at the nearby McCoy Cemetery. Nearly 2000 persons assembled at the graveyard on an

Lockhart's grave. Photo by Naomi Morgan.

unusually bitter cold afternoon to witness the burial, which included military honors provided by Sallisaw's Carnie Welch Post of the American Legion. Finally, after being moved from hither to yon for the past thirty-six hours, the charismatic outlaw's corpse was permanently laid to rest next to his father. A local reporter stated he overheard many in the somber crowd commenting how remarkable it was that Lockhart went to his death without killing a fellow human being in his career as an outlaw. If the remark was meant to serve as a defense for his wild and wicked ways, it was a feeble attempt, although the knowledge that he died devoid of the mark of Cain probably offered some comfort to his family.

On hearing the news of Lockhart's death, legendary US Marshal Alva McDonald commented, "He died like his associates, with his boots on in defiance of the law." J. A. Huff, a Pinkerton detective assigned to tracking down the nervy bandit stated in an interview with the McAlester News Capitol: "I just missed Ed at a whiskey still near Spavinaw the day before Grady got him, he got what was coming to him." Sequoyah County Sheriff John Johnson commenting on the outlaw's death, said, "Lockhart's downfall can directly be attributed to poker, fast women, and booze."

In the decade following the death of Ed Lockhart, there would be many pretenders to the throne, but until the arrival of another Sequoyah County man, Charles "Pretty Boy" Floyd, none (except possibly Matt Kimes) would be able to lay claim to the title "Bandit King" of

Ed Lockhart's death certificate. Courtesy Kenneth Butler.

Lockhart's prison record. Courtesy Oklahoma Department of Corrections.

the Southwest. Floyd, like Lockhart, would forever be remembered by a large segment of the rural working poor residing in the mountainous Oklahoma and Arkansas borderlands for his dash and charisma, and like his predecessor, he would die at the barrel of a lawman's smoking gun.

Once the excitement over Lockhart's death died down, it appears his brainy comrade-in-crime "Cotton" Walker, slipped back into the Cookson Hills seeking asylum with friends and family. In the weeks following the Sperry shootout, there was much talk of just how Officer Grady had discovered the whereabouts of the elusive Lockhart. One theory put forward by several area newspapers implied "Cotton's" relatives had informed on the elusive bandit due to his being partially responsible for Walker's prison escape. (Apparently, Lockhart had sent a correspondence to Walker in mid 1923 encouraging him to break out of jail and join him "on the scout.") According to Walker's kin, they had somehow arranged for him to be the recipient of an executive pardon, which was scheduled to go into effect only days after his untimely escape.

Chapter 10

Kaiser Bill, The Prairie Grove Caper, and Charley Misses a Cab

In early May 1924, the elusive "Kaiser" Bill Goodman was arrested under the name of Ira Hale in Kiowa County, Oklahoma on a charge of grand larceny. On May 28, the old bandit, who authorities had been attempting to capture since his 1918 escape from the Sequoyah County Jail where he was being held for the robbery of the Farmers Bank of Illinois in Gore, Oklahoma, was convicted and sentenced to five years on the larceny pinch. On his arrival at McAlester prison, the elderly desperado's true identity was discovered when a guard recognized him from one of his previous stays at the penal institution. Goodman (which was not his real name, just his favorite alias) was transported to Sallisaw where he was resentenced to his original 15 years for the Gore heist and given an additional five for his successful escape from the county jail. Adding to his troubles, soon after Goodman's identity was established, the state of Missouri began extradition hearings against the old thief due to his being wanted in the "Show Me" state on a vast array of charges. After Oklahoma's Governor turned down their extradition plea, Missouri officials settled on putting a hold on the bandit in case he was ever freed from the Oklahoma Penitentiary.

About the same time as "Kaiser" was being greeted by the welcoming committee at the state slammer, Bee Dotson, along with a notorious Sequoyah County character dubbed "Cowboy" Charley Cotner, so named for his amazing rodeo skills, were strolling into the First Na-

Copy of "Kaiser Bills" re-commitment papers, Sequoyah County. Courtesy Sequoyah County Clerks Office.

tional Bank of Prairie Grove, Arkansas, planning on making an unexpected withdrawal of funds. After looting the bank for $3550 in cash and bonds and locking cashiers S. J. Campbell and Will Pearson along with several witnesses into the vault, the duo jumped into a dilapidated Ford automobile reportedly driven by Bee's brother Charley and fled south. Within minutes of the robbery, several dozen Prairie Grove citizens who were later joined by Washington County Sheriff Sam Guinn and a group of his deputies formed a posse and began pursuing the bandits. At a point four miles southeast of town, the officers discovered the robber's abandoned getaway car suffering from two blown tires.

Bringing in a pack of bloodhounds, the officers and vigilantes were soon able to pick up the bandit's trail, which led deep into a rugged section of the Ozark Mountains. By walking nonstop through the night, the fugitives were just able to stay ahead of the posse. By dawn, they had covered nearly seven miles (much of it straight up and down). Deciding to take a break, the trio collapsed in an exhausted heap on the floor of a forested hollow, located near the head of Fall Creek.

Meanwhile, back with the posse, Deputy Sheriff Charles Birchfield decided to drive ahead of the others hoping to cut the bandit's trail near the small village of Strickler, Arkansas. Upon his arrival at the crossroads community, an eighteen-year-old youth named Hooper approached the lawman breathlessly informing him he had spotted the bank robbers in the nearby Fall Creek Hollow. Deciding to investigate, he accompanied the young man to the big gully where he spotted the resting fugitives. When the Deputy called on the trio to surrender, the bandits responded by peppering his position with a half-dozen rounds from their high-powered rifles. Armed with a .12 gauge pump shotgun, Birchfield traded shots with the fugitives until a 30-calibre slug exploded into his chest.

Seeing his comrade hit the ground, the officer's young companion threw up his hands in surrender. The outlaws approached the downed lawman while covering his partner with their guns. According to the youth, one of the trio (later identified as Charlie Cotner) nudged the wounded lawmen with the toe of his boot, before turning to the frightened youth saying "I believe we just killed old squirrel face here, you better go back home and tend your chickens if you don't want some of the same." With that said, the outlaws fled on foot in a northerly direction leaving the young man standing in the field. Luckily, the wounded officer survived. According to the tending physician, Dr. E. G. McCormick, the bullet missed his heart by less than an inch. The following day the robbers stole a Ford Touring car from Albert Reed, a farmer living near the Morrow community located roughly six miles due west from the site of the ambush on Deputy Birchfield. Lawmen soon traced the stolen automobile to the village of Summers where the trio had gassed up and ate breakfast before high tailing it back across the nearby Oklahoma border.

Nothing was heard of the Prairie Grove robbers until June 15 when a posse led by Sequoyah County Oklahoma Sheriff John Johnson, acting on a tip, located "Cowboy" Charlie Cotner at a rodeo near Sallisaw. Catching sight of the approaching posse, Charlie, who was entered in the bulldogging contest, immediately fled the arena, jumped a fence, ran through the crowded grandstand and dashed across a parking lot before bolting into a hay field trying to make his way to a patch of woods located several hundred yards away. Encouraged by the boisterous cheers of 5000 sunburned rodeo fans that thought the footrace was part of the act, the outlaw soon began outdistancing the pursuing lawmen. Tiring of the chase and motivated by a recently posted $500 "dead or alive" reward offered for the bandit's head on a platter, the officers soon stopped running and began throwing lead in the fugitive's direction. Caught in the middle of a large open pasture, Cotner, realizing he would likely be killed if he continued to flee, promptly threw up his hands in surrender. Prairie Grove banker, S. J. Campbell, who had accompa-

Mug shot, "Cowboy" Charley Cotner. Courtesy Ida Works, Arkansas Department of Corrections.

nied the officers on the raid, took one look at Cotner and promptly identified him as one of the robbers.

Shortly after Cotner's arrest, a gang of youths, who were reportedly pals of the suspect, assaulted two of the arresting officers. Deputy Sheriff Sam Benge suffered a knife wound in the melee. The following day, Sheriff Johnson was informed "Cotton" Walker had been sitting in the stands during the previous nights disturbance egging the rowdy lads on in their attack on the officers. The elusive outlaw apparently slipped away during the ensuing confusion. Johnson told a group of newsmen he believed Walker was probably attending the rodeo hoping to catch Cotner's performance.

Following his arrest, Cotner agreed to extradition and was transported to Fayetteville, Arkansas by Sequoyah County Deputies Cheek and Cotton to stand trial. Not only did witnesses from the Prairie Grove bank positively identify Cotner as a participant in that robbery, but a bank clerk from the recent Sulpher Springs, Arkansas bank robbery came forward fingering Cotner as one of the looters

Record of Charles Cotner's charges for "robbery and intent to kill."

of that institution as well. On June 30, 1924, the bandit pled guilty to both the robbery of the bank of Prairie Grove and the attempted murder of Deputy Birchfield. He was promptly sentenced to ten years hard labor at the Arkansas State Prison Farm in Tucker as inmate #21524. Incidentally, in the years following his 1930 release from prison, the colorful bandit would join the second so-called "Cookson Hills Gang" and make a name for himself as one of the most prolific bank robbers in the history of the American Southwest.

On the evening of September 23rd, seventeen-year-old Charley Dotson strolled up to a taxi driver sitting in his 1923 Dodge Brothers cab in downtown Vinita, Oklahoma, jamming a .32-20 Smith and Wesson pistol into his ribs and with a smirk on his face, ordered him to drive to Muskogee. The hack driver, Calvin MacDonald, waited until the lad had entered the cab sitting on the rear seat before stomping on the gas and getting the rig up to thirty miles per hour before intentionally slamming the vehicle into a brick wall next to the Short Line filling station.

Charles Dotson.
Courtesy Muskogee Phoenix.

When the taxi driver, who was apparently unfazed by the crash, attempted to leave the cab, the hijacker struck him repeatedly in the head with his gun barrel. MacDonald, with a trail of blood flowing from his wounds, began pleading for assistance from a gathering crowd of spectators. Dotson, infuriated by the lack of cooperation

KATY rail depot and hotel, Muskogee, Oklahoma, circa 1920.
Courtesy Three Rivers Museum, Muskogee, Oklahoma.

he was receiving, aimed his pistol at MacDonald and pulled the trigger. Nothing happened. The bandit, in his overzealous striking of the poor cab man had damaged the pistol's firing mechanism, rendering it useless. Faced with this unexpected development, Charley bolted from the cab and began running towards the town's rail yard

Court record Craig County Oklahoma vs. Charley Dotson.
Courtesy Craig County Clerks Office.

with the angry crowd, now grown to over a dozen citizens, hot on his heels. After sprinting like a scared deer for nearly half a mile, the young gunman finally out distanced his pursuers. When lawmen were informed of the aborted hijacking, a large posse of officers and volunteers began combing the edge of town where Dotson was last seen. Unfortunately, for the authorities, Charley was able to escape by hopping into an open boxcar of a conveniently passing southbound freight.

Dismounting the boxcar just outside the community of Pryor, Dotson footed it into town. On arrival at the passenger depot, he purchased a first class ticket to Muskogee. Meanwhile, Craig County officials suspecting the young man had caught a ride from either a passing automobile or freight train, contacted officials in Wagoner, Muskogee and Checotah to be on the lookout for the fugitive. At 4:30 am, two Muskogee city policemen, Patrolman Pete Hazen and Detective Ed Corbin, who were keeping an eye on passengers coming and going at Muskogee's KATY depot, arrested Dotson as he stepped off the train. When the officers attempted to search the youth, he suddenly pulled a pistol from his pocket while simultaneously jerking the trigger. When the gun failed to fire, Corbin yanked it from his hand before commencing to adjust the young man's attitude with his handy lead-filled blackjack.

Two hours later, two Vinita city cops steamed into town via rail, picking up their now well-mannered prisoner. On arrival back in Vinita, the cab driver, Calvin MacDonald, positively identified the lad as his attacker. Although the fugitive claimed his name was Robert Allen, Craig County Sheriff Harry J. Campbell quickly cried foul when he discovered a wanted poster of a Charles T. Dotson who was being sought in connection with Ed Lockhart's 1923 Jay, Oklahoma jailbreak as well as the recent robbery of the First National Bank of Prairie Grove, Arkansas. The likeness on the poster perfectly matched that of the young man in custody. Adding to the confusion, the Craig County Clerk came forward stating she had sold a marriage license to the prisoner on the morning of the hijacking. Dotson had purchased the license under the name of Roy A. Allen of Claremore, Oklahoma. The bride was listed as hailing from Pettit, Cherokee County, Oklahoma. After a bit more attitude adjustment, the adolescent criminal admitted his true identity.

Refusing to confess his guilt in the aborted hijacking, Dotson was put on trial, Craig County criminal case #1600, and was convicted of attempted robbery and assault to kill. District Judge A. C. Brewster hammered the youth with a hefty twenty-five-year sentence and $138.00 court costs. On November 23, 1924, Charley Dotson was received, inmate #14566, at the Oklahoma State Penitentiary.

Chapter 11

Firestorm over the Cooksons

The peace and quiet of the hills was broken on July 29, 1925, when four young area residents robbed and senselessly shot an elderly vacationer who was camping deep in the hills on the banks of the Illinois River, for a mere $3.10. The innocent victim, 68-year-old John Ogelsby, was a retired businessman from Henryetta, Oklahoma. After being wounded, Ogelsby was carried to the nearby home of a family named Jolliff where he lay unconscious on a cot for twenty-four hours before expiring. The public reaction to the old man's murder was one of great anger. Especially disturbed by the vile act were the state's many sportsmen who had long sought access to the secluded hills, attracted by the area's pristine fish choked rivers and abundant wildlife. Due to the recent publishing of several stories in a popular nationally syndicated outdoors magazine which touted the Cooksons as one of the finest outdoor recreational areas in the nation, sportsmen had been crowding into the district in droves. Many residents of the isolated hills were clannish and held a deep mistrust of outsiders. These folks resented the influx of foreigners, who they feared threatened their way of life. This clash of cultures was responsible for a sudden rise in ugly incidents between the hill folk and sportsmen. Unwilling to consider the negative impact on the area and its citizens, the Oklahoma Game and Fish Commission, had over the past several years spent considerable time and effort in promoting the area as a vacationer's paradise.

Oglesby's murder was a spark that ignited a firestorm. Due to public pressure, Oklahoma Governor "Alfalfa" Murray demanded area lawmen clean up the notorious hills. Sam Morley, director of the Game and Fish Commission was ordered by the state's Chief Executive to make the Cooksons safe for sportsmen. A squad of Oklahoma Bureau of Investigation operatives under L. C. Gish, as well as Mont Grady and a dozen armed state game wardens began infiltrating the Cooksons in hopes of flushing out Ogelsby's killers. Cherokee County Sheriff Jerry Powell and a group of his deputies soon joined them. The assortment of lawmen, detectives, and wardens were also handed a list of known bad men to be on the lookout for. Incidentally, scores of area residents vigorously assisted the crime fighters in their hunt for the elderly man's assassins. Although many inhabitants of the district were wary of the influx of sportsmen in the past few years, the vast majority condemned the perpetrators of the Ogelsby murder.

Sheriff Jerry Powell in later years. Courtesy Cherokee County Sheriff's Department.

In early August, the young "toughs" who were involved in the Ogelsby slaying were apprehended by Grady and a contingent of Cherokee County deputies. One of the youths admitted committing the actual murder while the others confessed they either watched or assisted. All were sent to prison ending the tragic affair. Also arrested in the sweep of the hills was eighteen-year-old Russell

King who confessed to aiding Fred Walker and Bee Dotson in carrying out the recent robberies of the Wauhillau, Lowery, and Cookson stores. When the youth informed lawmen he had been employed as a plow jockey on Mount Cookson's farm at the time of the robberies, Sheriff Powell ordered the thirty-six-year-old self-proclaimed "reformed bandit" picked up and charged with harboring. Although Cookson, who had recently been released from prison and was currently on parole, vehemently denied any knowledge of his hired hands criminal activities, the Governor was persuaded by Sheriff Powell and Cherokee County Prosecutor W. W. Miller to revoke his parole and order him back to McAlester. In all fairness, it appears the most likely explanation for Cookson's parole revocation seems not to have been due to his commission of any specific crime, but payment from the authorities for his alleged long-term association with Fred Walker.

The mention by the teenage suspect of Fred Walker and Bee Dotson in connection to the recent rash of rural store robberies in Cherokee county perked Mont Grady's interest. The lawman, along with Cherokee County Sheriff Powell, who possessed an intense dislike for "Cottontop," began a surveillance of the homes of the fugitive's friends and family.

****

In the early morning hours of August 9, Cherokee County Deputy Sheriffs E. S. Watkins and Tom Doolen were sitting in their Ford roadster keeping watch on the front door of the R. F. King Mercantile store in Hulbert. The business had been the victim of several recent break-ins. Suddenly the pair observed three individuals stroll up to the door and began working on it with a crowbar.

The lawmen leaped out of their rig shouting to the trio to "Give up you're under arrest." The burglars responded by firing several rounds from a pistol toward the lawmen. Watkins, struck by a slug in the arm fell to the ground. His partner reacted by unloading his revolver at the trio before pulling his partner to safety. The thieves jumped into a Ford Touring Car with Arkansas plates and with a squall of rubber, sped west. When a resident of a neighboring home showed up offering the lawmen assistance, Watkins instructed the "Good Samaritan" to phone the town marshal in the nearby community of Ray and instruct him to be on the lookout for the suspect's car which was heading his way. With that said, the wounded deputy and his partner hopped into their Ford Roadster and began pursuing the thieves. When the lawmen caught up with the hoodlums and attempted to force their rig off the road they were greeted with a volley of pistol fire, several rounds striking the roadster's radiator.

Upon receiving word of the Hulbert shooting, Ray Marshal Frank Redman drafted a young friend into assisting him. The pair immediately began driving at breakneck speed toward the main road hoping to cut off the fleeing yeggmen. Within minutes of establishing a roadblock at the highway junction, the fugitive's car came rushing past their position. Following close behind were the pair of Cherokee County lawmen in their sputtering roadster, water pouring from the damaged radiator. When the deputy's disabled car pulled adjacent to Redman's parked vehicle, the wounded Watkins leaped from the rig piling into the back seat with a shout of "Get going!" While Doolen stayed with their crippled roadster, Redman and his two passengers took up the chase.

After speeding through the town of Okay and into the north side of Muskogee, the fugitives turned east at the Mid-West Glass Casket Company and sped across the

Arkansas River Bridge toward Fort Gibson. The chase ended when the suspect's car was halted at a rail crossing by a passing freight train. Redman and his partners stopped a hundred yards behind the suspect's vehicle. The officers stepped from their car and cautiously approached the stalled vehicle, guns at the ready. When Watkins called out demanding the occupant's surrender, the suspects responded with a barrage of gunfire. Watkins in turn emptied his revolver into the car while Redman got off only a single round from his antique 1873 model Winchester .44-40 caliber rifle, before the contrary weapon hang fired. Suddenly, the driver of the rig pitched forward, slumping over the steering wheel. His companions, feeling the gig was up, baled out of the car fleeing on foot across a field towards nearby Braggs Mountain. Watkins, having to reload, quickly lost sight of the fugitives in the darkness and fog. Due to Marshal Redman's malfunctioning firearm, he was also forced to stand idly by as the fugitives fled across a nearby pasture. The marshal's youthful driver who was unarmed took no part in the shootout.

On approaching the suspect's stalled car, Watkins

Ford Model "T"s similar to those used throughout the story.
Courtesy Model "T" Club of Tulsa, photo taken by Naomi Morgan
at historic Dwight Mission, Oklahoma.

News headline noting Bee Dotson's death. Courtesy Muskogee Phoenix.

was able to identify the lifeless driver as the notorious Bee Dotson, who was wanted for a multitude of charges including the recent robberies of the banks of Prairie Grove and Sulpher City, Arkansas, along with the Cookson, Lowery and Wauhillau store heists. The daring bandit was also suspected of assisting in Ed Lockhart's jail delivery two years previously. He had been arrested and released on bond on the jailbreak charge, but had jumped bail and since been scouting.

Watkins, recovering from his gunshot injury, which proved to be a minor flesh wound, noted in his report that one of the six rounds he had fired from his .38 caliber pistol during the gun-duel had struck Dotson in the left eye and exited out his right ear, while the single rifle slug Officer Redman had fired, found paydirt glancing off Dotson's pocket watch before plowing a fatal path deep into the outlaw's heart.

Within minutes of the conclusion of the high-speed chase, Muskogee city officers arrived at the scene and began tracking the missing fugitives with bloodhounds. Mont Grady and Cherokee County Sheriff Powell, along with Muskogee County Undersheriff Roy Jones, Deputies Sam Benge, John Marlow, and R.A. Payne, later joined them. After trailing the fugitives for nearly fifteen miles, the lawmen and their pack of bloodhounds lost the track and gave up the chase.

Dotson's corpse was held at the Muskogee morgue for several days until the witnesses from two recent bank robberies arrived from Arkansas. It seems the authorities expected on collecting the $1000 a head "dead or alive" reward offered for the robbers of those institutions. On the morning of August 12, bank employees from both Sulpher City and Prairie Grove positively identified Dotson as one of the holdup men who had raided their respective businesses.

The following day, Bee Dotson was buried next to his father in the old Dwight Mission graveyard located just north of Vian, Oklahoma. The year 1925 had proved to be a tragic time for the Dotson's. Bee's Uncle Abe had been killed a month earlier in an argument over a jug of moonshine. It seems Abe had invited a young neighbor to accompany him to a local moonshine still, proposing the pair sample the goods. The youth refused the elder Dotson's request, saying he needed to "Tend his crops." Dotson, who was a renowned knife fighter, pulled a pig sticker from his back pocket and threatened to cut the boy from gut to gizzard if he didn't honor his request. Knowing the tough hill-man would do just what he promised, the terrified young man fled into a friend's home grabbing a double barrel shotgun that was hanging on a wall, turned and let the pursuing Dotson have it with a charge of buckshot in the chest. Staggering into the road,

Dotson fell to the ground with an audible groan. The shotgun wielding youth then approached his fallen victim and taking deliberate aim emptied the second barrel into his neck, damn near separating his head from his shoulders.

****

Meanwhile, Fred Walker, holed-up deep in his Cookson Hills lair, was deeply troubled by the reports of Bee Dotson's demise as well as Lockhart's death at the hands of Mont Grady. Even less appealing to him was the fact the lawman had slain his partner on his ex-wife's (she had since divorced him) doorstep. Knowing he had missed capture or death by a hairsbreadth at the time of Lockhart's death, and being fully aware his nemesis was currently "bird dogging" through the hills due to the Ogelsby murder investigation, he promptly got the word to his attorney, J. Berry King, requesting he contact Grady and make arrangements for his peaceful surrender. He also sent his .351 Winchester rifle and a Lugar pistol along to give to the lawman as a sign of his sincerity. Grady accepted the proposal, instructing the lawyer to have his client meet him in front of the Cherokee County courthouse in Tahlequah at noon the following day. At exactly 12, on August 21, 1925 "Cotton" Walker walked up to Grady on the courthouse lawn stretching out his hands in submission. When the lawman asked what motivated his surrender, the bandit retorted, "I'm tired of

Shared gravestone of Bee and Berry Dotson. Photo by Naomi Morgan.

being the fox to the hounds."

Instead of lodging his prisoner in the county jail, Grady and the outlaw checked into an area hotel where they rested up before the trip back to the penitentiary. The motivation behind this odd act appears to have been Walker's fear of Cherokee County Sheriff Powell who held the outlaw in utter contempt. This ill will stemmed from a recent exchange of correspondence between the lawman and the outlaw. Apparently, the Sheriff, who had also been involved in the 1922 manhunt for Walker and his fellow gang members when he was a deputy, had made a statement to a local newspaper, which implied he and his deputies intended on shooting the outlaw on sight, Walker and his cronies responded by sending word from the hills claiming they would gladly return the favor.

At the hotel, Walker gave an interview to a female reporter from the Muskogee Phoenix named Frankie Cornelius in which he loudly claimed he was driven to crime by "circumstances beyond my control," adding, "I surrendered in order to thwart the current county sheriff's plans to assassinate me." Naturally, he had nothing but high praise for his captor (Grady) who he claimed to deeply admire, saying, "Grady has treated me like a white man, his bloodthirsty reputation is unfounded." The bandit angrily denied any involvement with any of the individuals implicated in the Ogelsby murder, calling them "punks." Walker also stated, "Powell had no right to revoke Mount Cookson's parole, he was living like an honest citizen at the time and was pitched back into prison because he refused to rat on me. I only spoke to Mount once in the past year and have always thought of him as a brother and true friend."

When asked about Bee Dotson's untimely demise, Walker said, "Darn shame. I recently swapped a .45 Colts pistol to Bee for that .351 Winchester I turned into Grady."

"Cotton" surrenders Upper right: "Cotton" Walker to his left Mont Grady. Below: Walker, Phoenix reporter Frankie Cornelius, and Grady. Bottom: Lawyer J. Berry King. Courtesy of The Muskogee Phoenix.

The outlaw continued his discourse, saying, "Bee played no part in that Ogelsby killing." His rambling two-hour statement appears to have been mainly an exercise in expelling hot air. In the end, Fred Walker was a tragic figure, a man with a brilliant mind and imagination who

Headline stating the Cherokee Hills were cleaned up.
Courtesy The Muskogee Times.

wasted his talents in the selfish pursuits of his own comforts.

With Walker's incarceration in the Oklahoma State Penitentiary and Bee Dotson's death, the notorious band of highwaymen known to many as the original "Cookson Gang" came to an inglorious end. But in just a few short years, they would be replaced by an even deadlier group of bad men who would be dubbed the "Cookson Hills Gang" by the press. It is often said, "The more things change, the more they stay the same."

Epilogue

As for the fates of the leading characters noted in this book, I'll list what became of them to best of my knowledge.

MONT GRADY: In the months following the demise of the Cookson Gang, he was involved in a nationwide manhunt for the notorious Lawrence brothers. The pair had murdered three lawmen (including Muskogee County Oklahoma Deputy Sheriff Joe Morgan) in a five state, eighteen-month-long crime spree. The brothers were finally captured near Tempe, Arizona after gunning down Phoenix Patrolman Haze Burch (the first Phoenix officer to die in the line of duty). Grady went on to serve as a peace officer in the booming oil field town of Wewoka, Oklahoma, where he was involved in at least one shooting scrape. He was later employed in Tulsa as a hotel detective prior to serving as a plainclothes officer for the Tulsa Police Department. The noted manhunter succumbed to a liver ailment at Morningside Hospital in Tulsa on December 16, 1930. His body was transported to his hometown of Hartshorne by rail escorted by a contingent of Tulsa police officers. Grady was buried next to his first wife at the Elmwood Cemetery. Sadly, the legendary peace officer lies in an unmarked grave. Grady, who was known far and wide in the 1920s as one of the bravest and most efficient lawman to ever wear a badge in the Southwest, has since been nearly forgotten in the telling of Oklahoma law enforcement history.

SAM LOCKHART: Was captured shortly after he robbed a bank in Wewoka, Oklahoma on March 17, 1929. The errant bandit was sentenced to five years in the Oklahoma State Pen. A few months after his release from prison on December 7, 1931, he, along with notorious Bradshaw brothers were suspected of robbing the bank of Vian, Oklahoma. In 1933, he was convicted of robbing a bank in Logan County, Arkansas. After serving a five-year sentence, Sam moved to the state of Washington where he died in 1952. His body was shipped back to Fort Gibson, Oklahoma, where he was interred in the National Cemetery. He, like many of his comrades in the original "Cookson Gang," were veterans of the First World War.

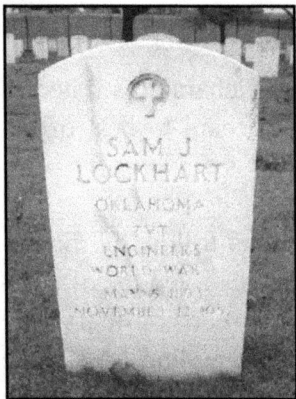

Grave of Sam Lockhart
Photo by Naomi Morgan.

Sam Lockhart's prison record. Courtesy of the Oklahoma Department of Corrections.

CHARLEY DOTSON: After his release from the Oklahoma State Penitentiary in the early 1930s where he had been a cellmate of the notorious Wilber Underhill, the handsome young outlaw became involved with the second Cookson Gang. In 1933, he was arrested for the robbery of the banks of Haskell, Oklahoma and York, Nebraska. Although his wife spent a small fortune in ill-gotten funds on his defense, the bandit was convicted and sentenced to twenty-five-years at the Nebraska State Penitentiary in early 1934. The colorful outlaw succumbed to the effects of T.B., which he had been suffering from since his earlier stay at the Oklahoma pen, after serving only a few months of his sentence. He rests near his father, brother, and uncle, who all three died violent deaths, at the Dwight Mission Cemetery near Marble City, Oklahoma.

Appeal placed in York, Nebraska newspaper during Charley's 1934 trial, paid for by Mrs. Charley Dotson. Courtesy York News-Times.

An Appeal

Any one who may have been near the First National bank on Sept. 20, the day it was robbed is urgently requested to get in touch with Calvin Webster, if by any chance he saw the four bandits, when they entered or left the bank.

Mrs. Charles Dotson has requested that this appeal be made in an effort to secure evidence which will tend to prove her husband's innocence and secure a new trial.

Grave of Charley Dotson. Photo by Naomi Morgan.

REECE AND WILLIAM PRICE: Died in 1947 and 1987 respectively. Both were buried near their brothers Charlie and George in the Buffington Cemetery in Sallisaw, Oklahoma.

Grave of William Price. Photo by Naomi Morgan.

Grave of Reece Price. Photo by Naomi Morgan.

BUSH WOOD: Died of T. B. in El Paso, Texas, on December 18, 1928. He is buried next to his mother in Muskogee's Greenhill Cemetery.

Grave of Bush Wood. Photo by Naomi Morgan.

RUFUS ROLLEN: Upon his parole from prison, Rollen moved back to the bosom of his family in Claremore, Oklahoma. After being cleared of suspicion in the Maize robbery, he was involved in a shooting scrape at an area barn dance. Several hours after the incident in question, Claremore police officers R. S. Hubbard and Guy Williams arrested him leaning against a lamppost on a downtown street corner in a state of extreme drunkenness. When the officers attempted to secure him in a cell at the local jail, he bolted out the buildings main door rushing onto the street. After ignoring a demand to halt, Hubbard shot Rufus in the kneecap. When the lawmen attempted to force the bleeding fugitive into a jail cell the second time, Rollen suddenly turned and smashed

Grave of Rufus Rollen. Photo by Naomi Morgan.

Hubbard with a right cross to the jaw. Officer Williams reacted by popping the agitated prisoner on the gourd with his pistol butt. That did the trick.

The ex-rodeo star spent the depression working at the Kansas City stockyards. He did not age gracefully; being twice convicted of felony crimes while in his early seventies and serving two more short sentences in the Oklahoma pen. Rollen passed away in Tulsa, Oklahoma on March 9, 1972, and is buried at Woodlawn Cemetery in Claremore, Oklahoma

KIE CARLILE: In October 1923, Carlile was convicted of looting the First State Bank of Ochelata, Oklahoma, and sentenced to twenty years imprisonment. After his 1931 escape from the Oklahoma pen, he robbed a pair of banks in Arkansas. He was soon captured and sentenced to the Arkansas Sate Penitentiary in Little Rock where he and a partner named Troy Love promptly

Grave of Kie Carlile (left) and Troy Love (below), Pettit, Oklahoma. Photo by Naomi Morgan.

escaped and fled back to the Cookson Hills and founded the second so-called Cookson Gang. After robbing a string of banks in Oklahoma and Arkansas, he, along with Love were killed in a spectacular gun battle with law officers in Cherokee County, Oklahoma in September 1932. Carlile and his pal were buried in a common grave at the Pettit, Oklahoma Cemetery.

MONROE COOK: Who robbed the Muldrow bank along with the Price brothers, died in California in early 1960's.

SHERIFF GEORGE GOURD: Died in 1931 and rests in the Moody Graveyard in Cherokee County, Oklahoma.

MARSHAL JIMMY (Nick) NICKOLSON: Died in of stomach cancer at the Indian Hospital in Claremore, Oklahoma on July 3, 1931, and is buried in Ramona, Oklahoma.

FRED "Cotton" WALKER: Was paroled from the Oklahoma State Penitentiary on October 6, 1929 and was immediately suspected of the October 9th robbery of the Farmers State Bank of Locust Grove, Oklahoma. After crawfishing out of the armed robbery charges, he reportedly took up residence near Siloam Springs, Arkansas where he went into the livestock business. According to local folklore, he helped plan several bank robberies in the early 1930s committed by the second so-called "Cookson Hills Gang." Rumor has it, the old bandit was still alive and well late into the 1950s.

BUD MAXFIELD: Henry Starr's longtime partner, who was captured with him in the aftermath of the 1915

Stroud, Oklahoma, bank robbery, was shot and killed by officers in a running gunfight on March 27, 1923. He, along with the notorious Al Spencer and several others had recently robbed the bank at Mannford, Oklahoma, of $600. Many lawmen suspected Maxfield had originally been slated to participate in the ruinous 1921 Harrison bank raid with Henry Starr and company, but pulled a no-show at the last minute.

CHARLIE BRACKETT: Was paroled from the penitentiary October 23, 1923. He died in 1926 at the age of thirty-nine of natural causes (possibly T.B.) and is buried at Caney Cemetery, Adair County, Oklahoma.

Grave of Charlie Brackett.
Photo by Naomi Morgan.

CURTIS HAYES: Was released from McAlester prison on October 15, 1923. He was arrested for suspicion of auto theft in the big February 1934 Cookson Hills raid conducted by nearly 1000 Lawmen and National Guardsmen. Hayes was released the following day and the charges dropped due to lack of evidence.

LEWIS CURTIS: The Park Hill robber was paroled from prison on December 18, 1922 after serving only nine months of his five year sentence. His wife divorced him and Lewis drifted off to Northwest Arkansas where he soon remarried. In 1930, he was listed on the census as the owner-operator of a shoe store located in downtown Springdale, Arkansas. Curtis remarried several times in the coming decades and sired a dozen children. He died in Arizona in the 1980s.

W. J. MYERS: The elderly bank director who slew Henry Starr during the Harrison bank robbery, died in 1936 and is buried in Harrison, Arkansas.

SHERIFF BOB SANFORD: Would serve two terms as Tulsa County Sheriff. In 1930, he was hired by the Tulsa City Police Department as a Desk Sergeant.

DEPUTY JAY FELLOWS: Left the Cherokee County Sheriff's department in the mid-1920s and went to work for the highway department.

HOMER E. BRITTIAN: The brave Arkansas lawman that faced down George Price on that stone stairwell in 1922, died on August 10, 1957 and was interred in the Eureka Springs Cemetery

ERNEST JORDAN: Another of the Eureka Springs defenders who engaged the Price brothers in mortal combat died in 1961 and was also buried at the Eureka Springs Cemetery.

MOUNT COOKSON: Was paroled from the Oklahoma pen in January 1926, his parole was revoked in 1931 due to his suspected involvement in a bootlegging ring. He was returned to prison and again paroled in February

Mount Cookson mug shot 1934 Tucker prison. Courtesy of Ida Works, Arkansas DOC.

1932. He was soon mixed-up with his brother-in-law "Kie" Carlile and the second Cookson Hills Gang. After serving a jolt in the Arkansas prison system in 1934-1940 for armed robbery, he was released and moved to Tulsa, Oklahoma where he died in the early '50s.

CHARLEY WHITE: After being arrested and released on a bootlegging charge in May 1932, he was implicated along with "Rabbit" Collins and "Willi Boy" Choate in the December, 1932 robbery of the Webbers Falls, Oklahoma, State Bank. Apparently, Choate and Collins had robbed the bank at gunpoint for roughly $1500. After the heist, the pair fled in a northerly direction driving a late model Oldsmobile, traveling to a point eight miles out of town on the "Moonshine Trail." The duo then abandoned the getaway car and waded the Illinois River before splitting up and going their separate ways. When the Oldsmobile was recovered the following day, investigators uncovered the fact the car was registered to Charley White. When questioned, White claimed the automobile had been stolen from his yard the night before the bank raid. Disbelieving him, authorities arrested Charley and charged him with hijacking the financial institution. After spending a week sleeping on a rock hard cot in the old Muskogee County jail, the local Judge released White for lack of evidence. When Choate was arrested in Tulsa on April 20, 1933, he confessed his part in the bank raid as well as implicating Collins as his partner in the actual robbery. He also claimed Charley White had allowed the pair to use his vehicle in the holdup for a $100 of the loot. Once again, Charley was arrested and charged with complicity in the robbery and locked up in the county jail without bail. Two weeks after Choate's capture, Collins surrendered to Muskogee County Sheriff V. S. Cannon saying, "I didn't want to be an outlaw all my life." He also confessed his involvement in the bank heist but refused to implicate White, instead suggesting he and "Willi Boy" had indeed stolen Charley's Oldsmobile. Soon afterwards, the pair pled guilty to armed robbery and both were sentenced to the state pen. In the end, the authorities in Muskogee lost interest in White's case and dismissed the charges. I suppose they figured two out of three ain't bad.

PERRY CHUCULATE: Was shot and killed by the notorious Kimes brothers on August 27, 1926, in a heated gun duel at a roadblock just west of Sallisaw, Oklahoma. After being convicted of Chuculate's murder and given a lengthy prison sentence, Mathew Kimes escaped from the Sequoyah County Jail and was destined to become a major crime figure in the Southwest. He participated in a series of dramatic bank robberies in both Oklahoma and Texas in 1926-7. Matt was captured in Arizona in 1927 and given a life sentence for the murder of Officer William McAnally in regards to a 1927 double bank robbery in Beggs, Oklahoma. The flamboyant outlaw bit the dust when he was run over by a poultry truck in North Little Rock, Arkansas, in 1945 while free on a temporary parole from the Oklahoma State Penitentiary.

Matt Kimes with Rev. Alton Parker at the Oklahoma State pen a few months prior to Kimes death. Incidentally, Parker preached Matt's funeral. Courtesy Tami Babione.

Dr. T. L. BALLENGER: The gutsy cashier from the Park Hill robbery quit the bank in 1923 and was appointed head of the history department at Northeastern State University in Tahlequah, Oklahoma. After his retirement in 1951, he wrote numerous articles for the Oklahoma Historical Society and authored the popular book, "Around Tahlequah Council Fires," dealing with Cherokee County history. He died in 1987 and is buried at the Tahlequah City Cemetery.

Dr. T. L. Ballenger late in life. Photo courtesy Tom Ballenger.

SHERIFF B.F. FAULKNER: Passed on in 1939 and was laid to rest in the little Akins Cemetery located in Sequoyah County, Oklahoma.

WILLIAM W. HASTINGS: Went on to serve nine terms in the US Congress. During his time in Congress, he worked diligently to bring better housing and medical care to Eastern Oklahoma as well as improving the area's transportation system. He died in 1938 and is buried at the Tahlequah City Cemetery.

J. Berry King. Courtesy Office of the Oklahoma Attorney General's Office.

J. BERRY KING: Fred Walkers one-time lawyer was appointed Oklahoma's state Attorney General by Governor W. J. Holloway in 1929. He served in that position until 1943.

WILLIAM S. KEY: Died in 1959. He spent most of his life in the corrections field. He also commanded the 45th U.S. Army Division in 1940 and retired a Major General.

William S. Key

"KAISER BILL" GOODMAN: Was paroled from the Oklahoma State Penitentiary on May 20, 1933. Somehow, the state of Missouri, who had placed a hold on the outlaw due to his being wanted in the state for several crimes including a parole violation, was not contacted about his release. At an age when most folks would retire to the rocking chair, the so-called "Fagin of the Hills" took on the awesome responsibility of personally instructing the wayward youths of the Cookson Hills in the fine art of bank robbery. On the morning of December 14, 1933, "Kaiser," along with Cliff "Kip" Harback and his tough, freckled faced, redheaded, cigar chomping girlfriend, Lillian Tackett, strolled into the Midland, Arkansas State Bank relieving the institution of $500. Cashier C. N. Finn described Goodman as elderly, bad tempered and foul mouthed. He added: "The younger bandit addressed the older man, who was armed with an old fashioned "chrome plated horse pistol," as "Dad." Two weeks later, the octogenarian bandit along with his pal Mount Cookson and three other individuals, thought to have been Ford Bradshaw, Robert Trollinger, and either "Cowboy" Charlie Cotner or "Kip" Harback, looted the National Bank of Mansfield, Arkansas, of nearly $700. Harback and Tackett were both captured on February 17, 1934 after Miss Tackett had shot the young gunsel in a domestic

First State Bank of Ketchum, Oklahoma, building is now a day care center. Photo by Naomi Morgan.

quarrel at a Hot Springs, Arkansas rooming house. After Harback recovered from his wound, he was sentenced to life imprisonment in connection with the May 29, 1933, slaying of a Paris, Arkansas banker and sent to Tucker Prison where he was fatally shot by officers while attempting to escape from the notorious institution on the evening of May 2, 1934. Miss Tackett, who appears to have been a classic gunman's moll of the period, was convicted of participating in the Midland robbery and sentenced to fifteen years in the Arkansas Women's Reformatory.

At 10:30 am. July 12, 1934, two men, one described as a youth, the other "aged' entered the First State Bank of Ketchum, Oklahoma. On duty at the time was a thirty-two year old Assistant Cashier named Luther Gregory, son of the banks president Ealum Gregory. The bank had not been robbed since 1923 when a trio of hoodlums had unsuccessfully raided the institution, killing cashier Frank Pitts in the process.

According to a statement given by Luther Gregory the day after the event: "The older man walked up to me at the counter asking how things were going before whipping out a big ivory handled pistol and ordering me to,

'Reach for the sky'. I was then instructed to lie on the floor. While he was scooping up the cash, a younger fellow held a automatic pistol on me." After looting the bank of approximately $300, the pair took Gregory hostage, forcing him into the front seat of their idling four-door sedan. The bandits freed their captive at a spot roughly three quarter of a mile south of the town limits. Upon his release, young Gregory turned and ran as fast as he could back to the bank where he rounded up his dad and an employee of the bank named Oscar Blackford. After arming themselves, the trio hopped in Luther's 1932 Chevy Coup and began pursuing the robbers.

Meanwhile, upon being notified of the heist, a half-dozen heavily armed posses took to the field, scouring the countryside. Within minutes of the robbery, a description of the bandits escaping car was broadcast on area radio stations. Over the next hour, the robbers were spotted traveling southwest of Ketchum, then doubling back east.

At straight up noon, the car containing the Gregory's and their companion topped a hill a mile south of Grove, near Honey Creek. Just ahead, they noticed a car parked on the side of the road that matched the description of the outlaw's vehicle, except it was sporting different tags. Three men were standing near the car talking. Slowing down to take a look, the younger Gregory who was driving, pulled abreast of the rig. Ealum Gregory, sitting in the front passenger seat, began opening the cars door that faced the suspicious vehicle, when suddenly an individual recognized as the old man from the robbery thrust a long-barreled pistol toward him firing two rounds before his gun misfired. While his partner was fiddling with his defective handgun, the younger bandit joined in the fray spraying down the bankers rig with an automatic pistol. After seeing his wounded father slump deep into his seat,

Guns used in Grove shootout, ivory handled six-shooter belonged to "Kaiser Bill," bottom, Colt automatic was used by Luther Gregory, Sr. to slay the noted bandit. Photo by Naomi Morgan.

Luther, whose heart must have been pounding about two hundred times a minute by this time, responded by firing several rounds from his Colt .32 cal. automatic pistol at the gray-haired attacker. The old man immediately tumbled to the ground fatally struck by two bullets in the

Luther Gregory Jr. with both guns used in deadly gun-duel near Grove, Oklahoma. Photo by Naomi

head. Gregory then turned and shot the third individual, who turned out to be an innocent bystander named H. T. Bradley, in the leg. Meanwhile, sitting in the coups rumble seat, Oscar Blackford, armed with a .351 rifle cut loose on the younger outlaw, shooting him in the chest and head. When the smoke cleared, three lifeless bodies lay sprawled on the roadway. Three men dead for a measly $300.

Within minutes of the shootout, a posse led by Craig County Sheriff John York arrived on the scene. Upon searching the pockets of the slain bandits, the stolen $300 was recovered along with three pistols, a high-powered rifle and a stolen set of license plates, which the bandits were in the process of changing when the Gregory car encountered them. An ambulance was called from nearby Grove and the bandit's bodies were transported to the Luginbuel Funeral Home in nearby Vinita where efforts to identify the robbers began.

After a laborious investigation, Sheriff York announced the identity of the elderly bandit as John R. Goodman, alias "Kaiser Bill," also known as "The old man of the hills," or the "Fagin of the Cooksons." The car the bandits were driving was identified as registered to a "relative" of "Cowboy" Charley Cotner's living in Vian, Oklahoma. Information quickly began coming into the Sheriff's office from a three state area indicating the old man was the chief suspect in a host of robberies committed over the past year. Prosecutors in nearby Tulsa County announced the picturesque bandit was wanted there for allegedly hijacking four rural grocery stores in the past sixty days. The state of Arkansas claimed the outlaw had definitely knocked over the Midland bank and was presumed to have had a hand in the December 30, 1933, Mansfield bank job. Kansas's authorities wanted him in connection to the armed robberies of several small businesses in their state as well. Officials at the Oklahoma, Arkansas, and Missouri State Penitentiaries all indicated the bad man had done time in their respective institutions. Sheriff Dee Watters of Ottawa County, Oklahoma, issued a statement to the press saying, "This Goodman, if that was his real name, has been a notorious scourge in these parts since before statehood." Federal officials at Leavenworth Federal Penitentiary announced Goodman had served at least two terms in their institution. Due to his liberal use of aliases, and lengthy career, which had began long before the use of fingerprinting; it was suspected he had actually done more time in the Federal prison system than they could find record of.

In the days following the bloody gunfight, the small town of Ketchum grieved for their fallen banker, Ealum Gregory, and celebrated the bravery of his son. The senior Gregory, who had been a respected leader of the community, and one of the founders of the victim bank, was buried in a solemn ceremony at the Ketchum Cemetery.

On July 19, Craig County officers announced the identity of "Kaisers" cohort as twenty-two-year-old Bill Quinton of Tahlequah, Oklahoma; unlike his crime partner, he had no previous record. Several days later, the lad's father showed up at the Burckhalter Funeral Home, where the young man's body had since been moved. Upon viewing his son's lifeless corpse, he said: "yep, that's him." Finding no family members willing to claim his body, "Kaiser Bill" Goodman, the last active "horseback" bandit of the wild-west era was interred in paupers grave #84 in Vinita's Fairview Cemetery at county expense. There were reportedly no mourners at the graveside.

Chronology Of Robberies

1918

- September 8: Farmers State Bank of Illinois at Gore, Oklahoma, robbed of $3,076 by means horseback. Suspects were Mount Cookson, Fred Walker, and "Kaiser" Bill Goodman.

1919

- December 5: Unsuccessful attempt to rob Citizens State Bank at Gans, Oklahoma, by means of horseback. Suspects were: "Kaiser" Bill Goodman and Bush Wood.

1920

- October: Farmers State Bank of Gore, Oklahoma, robbed of $2,000 by means of horseback. Suspects: "Kaiser" Bill Goodman, Bush Wood, possibly assisted by Fred Walker and Mount Cookson.

- December 20: Bank of Seligman, Missouri, robbed of $1,232 by means of an automobile. Suspects: Henry Starr, Ed Lockhart, Charlie Brackett, and possibly Rufus Rollen.

1921

- February 18: Unsuccessful attempt to rob Peoples National Bank of Harrison, Arkansas, by means of an automobile. Suspects: Henry Starr, Ed Lockhart, Charlie Brackett, and Rufus Rollen.

- April 25: Unsuccessful attempt to rob First State Bank of Locust Grove, Oklahoma. by means of an automobile. Suspects: Charlie Brackett, Bush Wood, Curtis Hayes, probably aided by Fred Walker and Ed Lockhart.

- December 20: Farmers State Bank of Illinois at Gore, Oklahoma, robbed of $1,600 by means of horseback. Suspects: Ed Lockhart, Jack Brody or Brodie

- December 20 (same day): Bank of North Arkansas at Everton, Arkansa,s robbed of $4,000 by means of horseback. Suspects: Sam Lockhart, L.W. Sitton, and George "Jack" Jackson.

1922

- January 20: First National Bank of Hulbert, Oklahoma, robbed of $2,300 by means of horseback. Suspects: Charlie, Will, and George Price, assisted by Fred Walker and Ed Lockhart.

- January 25: Farmers State Bank of Park Hill, Oklahoma, robbed of $570 by means of horseback. Suspects: Lewis Curtis and Charley White, assisted by Fred Walker and others.

- February 9: Adair State Bank, Adair, Oklahoma, robbed of $1,500 by means of automobile. Suspects: Tom Dodd, B. A. Robbie, Fred Walker, George and Charlie Price, and Berry Dotson. The robbery was never solved.

- June 2: First National Bank of Muldrow, Oklahoma, robbed of $17,000 by means of horseback. Suspects: Charlie and Reece Price along with Monroe Cook.

- September 17: Unsuccessful attempt to rob by means of automobile the National Bank of Eureka Springs, Arkansas, Suspects: George and Charlie Price, Si Wilson, John Cowan and Mark Hendricks, possibly assisted by Ed Lockhart and "Jack" Jackson.

- November: Farmers and Merchants Bank of Mountain Home, Arkansas, robbed of $2,000 cash and $1,550 in Liberty bonds by means of automobile Suspects: Ed and Sam Lockhart along with Artie Pendergrass.

1923
- August 22: Southern State Bank of Maize, Oklahoma, robbed of $1,644 by means of automobile. Suspects: Frank Rucker and, Bill Trotter, possibly aided by Rufus Rollen.

1924
- February 1: First National Bank of Shidler, Oklahoma, robbed of $2,000 by means of automobile. Suspects: Ed Lockhart, Bee Dotson, and possibly Bush Wood.

- May 19: First National Bank of Prairie Grove, Arkansas, robbed of $3,550 by means of automobile. Suspects: Bee and Charles Dotson, and Charley Cotner.

- June 1924-July 1925: Raids on banks of Sulpher Springs and Cave Springs, Arkansas. Store robberies in Wauhillau, Marble City, Cookson, Lowery and Hulbert, Oklahoma, Suspects: Mount Cookson, Fred Walker, Russell King, and Bee Dotson.

Sources

Newspapers:
The Daily Oklahoman, Oklahoma City, Oklahoma
Sallisaw Democrat-American, Sallisaw, Oklahoma.
Sequoyah County Democrat, Sallisaw, Oklahoma
Vinita Leader, Vinita, Oklahoma
Tahlequah Arrow-Democrat, Tahlequah, Oklahoma
Muskogee Times-Democrat, Muskogee, Oklahoma
Muskogee Phoenix, Muskogee, Oklahoma
Okmulgee Daily Times, Okmulgee, Oklahoma
Bartlesville Daily Enterprise, Bartlesville, Oklahoma
Haskell News, Haskell, Oklahoma
Tulsa Daily World, Tulsa, Oklahoma
Tulsa Tribune, Tulsa, Oklahoma
Fayetteville Daily Democrat, Fayetteville, Arkansas,
Joplin Globe, Joplin, Missouri
Fort Smith Southwest American, Fort Smith, Arkansas
Boone County Headlight, Harrison, Arkansas
Hartshorne Sun, Hartshorne, Oklahoma
Stroud Messenger, Stroud, Oklahoma
The Cherokee Advocate, Tahlequah, Oklahoma
The Arkansas Gazette
Claremore Progress, Oklahoma

Books:
Shirley, Glen, *Henry Starr: Last of the Real Badmen*,
    David McKay Co. Inc., N.Y.

Tolle, Edwin and Hatfield, Kevin: *The Great Eureka Springs Bank Robbery*. Eureka Springs Historical Museum.

Franks, Kenny A.; *The Osage Oil Boom*, 1989, Oklahoma Heritage Association.

Lamb, Arthur A.: "Tragedies of The Osage Hills" "Heritage of the Hills": A Delaware County History.

Faulk, Odie B., Jones, Billy M.: "Tahlequah, N.S.U. and the Cherokees," Northeastern State University, Tahlequah, Oklahoma.

West, C.W, *Outlaws and Peace Officers of the Indian Territory,* Muskogee, Oklahoma Publishing Company.

West, C. W. "Dub": *Tahlequah and the Cherokee Nation*, Muscogee Publishing Co., Muskogee, Oklahoma, 1978.

Call, Cora Pinkley, *Pioneer Tales of Eureka Springs*, Eureka Springs Historical Museum.

Periodicals:

Butler, Kenneth, "Ed Lockhart, an Outlaw From Sallisaw," *Oklahoma State Trooper Magazine*, Winter 2002.

Rayburn, Otto, "The Eureka Springs Story," *Times Echo Press*, Eureka Springs, Arkansas, 1954.

Westphal, June and Osterhage, Catherine, "A Time Not Easily Forgotten," *River Road Press*, Conway, Arkansas, 1970.

Koch, Mike, "The Life and Times of Henry Starr," *Oklahombres Journal*, Vol.14, Fall 2002.

Haser-Harris, Diane B, "Horse Racing in Oklahoma," *Chronicles of Oklahoma*, Volume LXIV, No. I, Spring 1986

Hodges, Bert, "Henry Starr's Last Holdup," *Lake Eufaula Fun News,* Oklahoma, June 1966, includes extracts from several interviews with survivors of Harrison, Arkansas robbery.

Brown, Horace B., "Death Trap" *Startling Detective*, 1923

Achieves-Facilities-Assistance:

Carnegie Public Library, Eureka Springs, Arkansas

Northeastern State University Library, Tahlequah, Oklahoma

Muskogee Public Library, Muskogee, Oklahoma

Fort Smith Public Library, Fort Smith, Arkansas

Okmulgee Public Library, Okmulgee, Oklahoma

Sallisaw Public Library, Sallisaw, Oklahoma

Muldrow, Public Library, Muldrow, Oklahoma

Vinita Public Library, Vinita, Oklahoma

Eureka Springs Historical Museum, Arkansas

Tulsa County Sheriff's Department, Tulsa, Oklahoma

Cherokee County Sheriff's Department, Tahlequah, Oklahoma

Craig County Sheriff's Department, Vinita, Oklahoma

Muskogee County Sheriff's Department, Muskogee, Oklahoma

Sequoyah County Sheriff's Department, Sallisaw, Oklahoma

Delaware County Sheriff's Department, Jay, Oklahoma

Mayes County Sheriff's Department, Pryor, Oklahoma

Oklahoma Department of Corrections

Arkansas Department of Corrections, Ida Works

Sequoyah County Court Clerks Office

Cherokee County Court Clerks Office

Muskogee County Court Clerks Office

Mayes County Court Clerks Office

Delaware County Historical Society and Museum, Jay, Oklahoma

Stroud Public Library, Stroud, Oklahoma

Stroud Chamber of Commerce, Oklahoma

Burckhalter Funeral Home, Vinita, Oklahoma

Luginbuel Funeral Home, Vinita, Oklahoma

Harrison Chamber of Commerce, Harrison, Arkansas

Claremore Public Library, Claremore, Oklahoma

www.ingramcontent.com/pod-product-compliance
Lightning Source LLC
Chambersburg PA
CBHW072132270326
41931CB00010B/1742